NO MALICE

NO MALICE

MY LIFE IN BASKETBALL

OR

How a Kid from Queensbridge Survived the Streets,
the Brawls, and Himself to Become an NBA Champion

METTA WORLD PEACE

with Ryan Dempsey

TRIUMPH
B O O K S

Library of Congress Cataloging-in-Publication Data
    Names: World Peace, Metta, 1979– author. | Dempsey, Ryan, 1977– collaborator.
    Title: No malice : my life in basketball, or, how a kid from Queensbridge survived the streets, the brawls, and himself to become an NBA champion / Metta World Peace, with Ryan Dempsey.
    Description: Chicago, Illinois : Triumph Books LLC, [2017]
    Identifiers: LCCN 2017023037 | ISBN 9781629374031
    Subjects: LCSH: World Peace, Metta, 1979– | Basketball players—United States—Biography. | Basketball—United States—History—20th century.
    Classification: LCC GV884.W6744 A3 2017 | DDC 796.323092 [B] —dc23 LC record available at https://lccn.loc .gov/2017023037

This book is available in quantity at special discounts for your group or organization. For further information, contact:
    Triumph Books LLC
    814 North Franklin
    Chicago, Illinois 60610
    (312) 337-0747
    www.triumphbooks.com

Printed in U.S.A.

ISBN 978-1-62937-403-1

Design by Sue Knopf

Photos courtesy of the author unless otherwise indicated

*To my mom, for impressing upon me
the value of making things fun,
and to my dad, for showing me the importance
of doing things right.*

Contents

Foreword

I had just been named coach of the Los Angeles Lakers in 1999 when we had Ron Artest and three other draft-eligible players come in to work out with our staff. I sat in on an interview with Ron after the workout, and I asked him why he was coming out of St. John's after only his sophomore year. He told me he had a responsibility to his family and that he had a steady girlfriend. What I learned from that interview was that even though he presented this warrior attitude on the basketball court, Ron had a naïve, innocent nature about him that was endearing.

Ron was the 16th pick in the first round by the Chicago Bulls, a team I had coached through the 1990s. I closely watched his progress as a professional. He was selected to the NBA's All-Rookie Team. He was traded to the Indiana Pacers a couple years later in a multi-player trade. While he was with the Pacers, he had success and helped the team. However, in 2004 he was involved in an ugly situation that ended with Ron in the stands fighting with a fan and getting suspended for the rest of the season. It could have been devastating to a player's career, but Ron was able to rehabilitate his life as an NBA player and as an adult.

After winning a title in 2009 with the Lakers, I was headed to Montana when I received a call from our GM, Mitch Kupchak. He told me that after running into difficult contract negotiations with our starting small forward, Trevor Ariza, the Lakers were going to sign Ron as a free agent. What did I think? I thought it was amazing that what goes around comes around, a simple fact of life. After watching Ron for 10 years through the ups and downs of his career, he was now going to be one of the players I got to coach.

Ron came with all the accolades and blessings of his reputation: tough defense, good team play, the ability to create steals, and the desire to win. The system of basketball we played in L.A. had the reputation of being difficult to learn, especially for older players with ingrained habits. Ron took to the learning experience with a beginner's mind and mastered playing alongside his teammates.

Playing the 2010 season as reigning champions was difficult. The years following a title can be tough; everyone is ready to challenge the champs. Ron came with the attitude: "You guys were champs, I'm just trying to help you win another one." He was always surprising me with his off-the-cuff behavior. He once stopped in front of the bench during a game and asked me to take him out as play continued up the floor. It was unusual for a player to ask for a substitution, as most guys resist coming out of a game. After the game I asked him why he'd asked, and he told me that his replacement was playing better than he was. First time for everything with Ron, but that taught me a lot about how he viewed his place on a team.

The Lakers with Ron as a starting forward won the 2010 NBA Finals against the Boston Celtics. It was a seven-game series and Ron played an important role in guarding the Celtics' top scorer, Paul Pierce, who had been instrumental in their win versus the Lakers in 2008. It was a knockdown series with hard play that exhausts teams. We struggled through a very difficult seventh game to win. I spoke to the press after it was over and said that I thought Ron was the most valuable player for us in that decisive game.

Ron/Metta has a lot of pride in being a part of the Lakers championship team, but it would probably take second place to his winning the J. Walter Kennedy Citizenship Award in 2011. Ron had to work through mental health issues during his tenure as an NBA player, and began to talk about it publicly and spoke in various forums about his experiences. His message was that being a big strong person doesn't mean that you can't struggle with mental illness. In Ron's post-championship speech to the press, he thanked his psychologist for helping him relax during the anxiety of the seventh game. This was a real positive moment for all of us who had watched Ron/Metta's career over the last 20 years.

I was recently at the last game Metta played at Madison Square Garden in New York City. He had played a season with the Knicks in 2013–14 and the fans cheered him as the buzzer sounded. He loved it and applauded the fans right back. He also was feted in his last game of the season with the Lakers. His career as an impact player was recognized as well as his longevity, but his ability to remain humble, approachable, and very grateful for his career touched the fans.

There are a lot of players who have been affected by the glamour of playing in the NBA, some in a negative way and some in a positive way. Metta World Peace has kept growing and expanding his education and his life through it all. His story is one for kids and adults to admire.

Phil Jackson won two NBA championships as a player with the New York Knicks, and 11 more as head coach of the Chicago Bulls and Los Angeles Lakers. He coached Metta World Peace in L.A. from 2009 to 2011.

Introduction

There is a solution to every problem. The solution may not be easy, but it's out there. You just have to find it. There are people who will tell you that you can't do certain things or that something's impossible because of who you are or where you come from. Growing up where I did, it's easy to think like that, but it's not true. I always wanted to do something that someone said was impossible. If I didn't think like that when I was younger, I never would have gotten to where I am today. When faced with any problem, you just have to figure out the solution in order to be successful.

That is what drew me to math as a kid, because in math every problem has a solution. Math was definitely a challenge for me, but that's what I liked about it. It also kept me occupied by something positive when I could have easily been occupied by something negative. There were times when I would walk over to 12th Street in Queensbridge and just work on my math homework. It has always been one of my favorite subjects. My junior high school math teacher was a hard-ass, but he taught me well and I enjoyed his class. It felt like he really wanted us to learn. He inspired me to want to become a junior high math teacher—growing up, that was my first goal. I knew that I wanted to play basketball, but I figured that I could make my living as a teacher.

Today, I still apply math to everything I do. I rely on math when it comes to my business and even when playing basketball—especially on defense. I like to look at the angles. I measure the distance between me and my man. I look at his feet and the ball and then change angles to make sure the center of my body is between my opponent's feet and the ball. If he's holding the ball out away from his body, I have to adjust to that. Being able to judge that distance is what helped me rack up more steals.

The problems I faced didn't get any easier as I got older, but the solutions were always out there. I had to figure out how to be able to run and keep up with these young boys out on the court. That meant changing my ways. Not drinking was one solution. When I was struggling in the playoffs with the Lakers, I'd meet with my psychologist. Together we found a solution to what was bothering me, and for those of you who watched Game 7 of the 2010 NBA Finals, you know how that turned out.

That NBA championship was a long time coming, and nothing could have prepared me for the road it took to get there. Earlier in my career it looked like I had the world at my feet. Going into the 2004 season with the Indiana Pacers, I was a possible MVP candidate. The previous year I was the Defensive Player of the Year and an All-Star. We were thinking NBA championship in Indiana, and I was off to a great start that season. Then everything changed in the final minute of a game against the Detroit Pistons that November.

Before I knew what happened, I had been suspended for the rest of the year. I lost $5 million. I lost all of my endorsements. No more sneaker deals. No more awards. All my commercials came off the air. That shit was over. I was in a real bad situation, but I had to move on. I had to work on finding the solution.

This isn't a book about all of the things that went wrong in my life. And I'm certainly not going to complain because a lot of people have gone through much worse.

Yes, I'm going to talk about the brawl in Detroit.

Yes, I'm going to talk about applying for a job at Circuit City when I played for the Chicago Bulls.

Yes, I'm going to talk about the fights and my temper and the suspensions and all the other things that have happened during my career.

I've faced a lot of problems. They've been well publicized, and a lot of them have been my own damn fault, but that's not what's important.

What's important are the solutions I found to help me overcome those problems.

QUEENSBRIDGE

Chapter 1

The Bridge

I grew up in the Queensbridge Housing Projects in Long Island City. If you've ever driven over the Queensboro Bridge from Manhattan, you can see those grayish-brown buildings shaped like two Ys connecting at the base. It's the largest housing project in North America. Twenty-nine apartment buildings with 96 units in each spread out over six blocks. I'm told there are more than 7,000 people living in more than 3,000 apartments and that first number is still growing. When I was a kid in the 1980s and '90s, the neighborhood was strictly black and Puerto Rican, but now it's more ethnically diverse.

The projects gave families an opportunity to survive, and for that it was a good thing, but it was also a breeding ground for drugs and violence. In 1986 there were more murders committed in Queensbridge than in any other New York City housing project. That's not a place you want to call home. Today I think of Queensbridge more as a place for shelter, but growing up as kids we didn't know any better. It never felt like we had to get out of there. The drugs and the violence were just a part of everyday life. We didn't fully understand the repercussions of selling drugs because that's just the way things were. That was normal.

Black people who grew up in more fortunate circumstances are quick to judge those who grew up in impoverished areas. Those are the people who say, "Metta is crazy." But I bet if those same people grew up in the environment I did, they would end up the exact same way I did. For all the good and the bad, I am who I am today because of what I experienced on those six blocks in Queensbridge.

My dad was the original Ronald Artest. He was born in Brooklyn but did most of his growing up in Philadelphia. He played a little ball in high school and then joined the Navy. He bounced around before returning to New York in 1977. He married my mom, Sarah, and on November 13, 1979, they gave birth to me—Ronald Artest Jr. Dad got a job at a hospital serving food and my mom worked as a bank teller. There wasn't a lot of money to go around, but we figured it out. We always found a way to make it work. We had tough times as a family, but we also had a lot of fun.

I have a big family. I've got 10 brothers and sisters. I've got 40 nieces and nephews, and five great-nieces and -nephews. I'm only 38 years old as I'm writing this. That right there tells you I'm from the hood. Sometimes we had 15 people living in our first apartment on 10th Street. My mom had three daughters before she even met my dad: Shalice, Shaundlyn, and Latoya. When they got older, they had kids who also lived with us.

My older sisters looked out for me, and we rode the bus to school together when I was young, which I thought was the coolest thing. I was closest to Shaundlyn. She took care of me. She also had the best room. My room was a mess, but her room was always clean. She had a bunch of CDs I could listen to and she had an air conditioner. She always let me sleep on her bed. That became my getaway.

I shared a room with my four brothers. That's probably why it was always a mess. Daniel and Isaiah are my two younger brothers and they have the same parents as me. Wally and Khalik are actually my cousins, but I call them my brothers. They're my aunt's kids on my father's side. Wally is three years older than me and came to live with us when I was 10, because my aunt was an unfit mother and got sent to the psych ward. Khalik is younger, and my parents took him in right after he was born.

With so many people living in the house there was always something going on. There was always a lot of music being played. My parents listened to R&B. My mom used to always play her records on Sunday. Her "Sunday Classics," that's what she called them. She'd play music by Marvin Gaye, Barry White, Luther Vandross, Teddy Pendergrass, and Anita Baker. It was all peaceful and relaxing—a far cry from the type of music that was coming out of the neighborhood.

When I was young I was a Michael Jackson fan. I wanted to dance like Michael. I had no idea that the richest legacy in hip-hop was all around me. In the 1980s and '90s we had MC Shan, Marley Marl, and Mobb Deep coming up in the area, but I didn't even know who those guys were. Tragedy dated one of my sisters, but I didn't know he was a rapper. Hostile and Screwball hung around with another one of my sisters, but I didn't know they were rappers. Capone from C-N-N was my third cousin. Every weekend I was at Nature's house. I didn't know the dude rapped because I was never into street shit like that. We just used to go to his house to watch WrestleMania and get us some Hostess Cakes. Nature's mom always had the goodies.

It wasn't until I turned 15 that I was like, "Oh shit, Mobb Deep is from Queensbridge." That same year Nas' *Illmatic* dropped. I had never seen Nas in the hood, but he grew up on 12ᵗʰ Street right around the corner from me, and now people were saying he was one of the best rappers of our time. That was amazing to me.

Even when I learned more about it, I never wanted to rap myself. I was never interested. I'd write rhymes but I did it for fun. My dad would help me out. It was funny to hear him because he sounded like a preacher. Now, whenever I bring people back to the neighborhood to show them around, I always refer to where we are by saying, "This is Nas' block," or "This is Mobb Deep's block."

The streets were known for being tough, but it was also a war zone inside my house. My parents fought constantly. I didn't even know what they were fighting about most of the time, but they were both doing stupid shit. Mom was flipping on Dad and Dad was flipping on Mom. Whenever things got physical, I got nervous. One time it got so bad that I thought one of them was going to get really hurt. Shalice must have seen the look in my eye because she took me by the arm and led me into her room. I sat on her bed and she handed me a magazine. There was a crash from the other room. The wall shook and we heard glass break, but Shalice remained calm and turned up the music to drown out the chaos. She'd act like nothing was wrong.

"Tell me what you did today," she'd say.

We'd sit there and talk. Even then I was aware of what she was doing, but it made me feel better anyway. My sisters always made me and my brothers feel safe. When my parents were done fighting, we'd go make sure Mom was straight. We were always close as a family, but that was just another way us kids all stuck together.

Between my parents fighting and all the violence out in the street, I grew up living in survival mode. I was a pretty good kid and I didn't get into any real trouble, but I couldn't seem to avoid fights. It's not like I went out looking for them—I swear that I never initiated a single confrontation. I only fought when I had to. That said, I did have a temper. I think I got that from my dad. His mom was also an angry person so maybe it was in our blood.

The earliest fight I can remember being in was back when I was in second grade. This kid tried to cut in front of me in the lunch line. I didn't know who he was. He was smaller than me, but he was acting like I wasn't even there. That got me mad. The line was long. I had been waiting for a while.

"What are you doing?" I asked.

At first he laughed and then he said, "This is my spot now." He turned around and ignored me.

"You better not think you're gonna cut in front of me."

"What are you gonna do?"

As soon as he said that, I snapped. My hands went right for his throat. He clawed back. I hit him. The teachers jumped in quick to break us apart. It was back to the principal's office for me.

I wasn't only getting in trouble at school. Even when I was with my own family, I sometimes found myself in survival mode. My family used to have cookouts in the park. Everyone would show up. We'd grill, eat out, and just spend the day there. These were usually laid-back gatherings, but one time I got into an argument with my sister over something stupid. Out of nowhere, my cousin Adam jumped in and started needling me.

"Why are you acting like a bitch?" he said.

"I'm not acting like a bitch, mind your business."

I tried to leave, but he kept following me.

"That's why you're walking away. Because you're a little bitch."

I knew he was joking, that he was trying to get under my skin, but it was working.

"I'm not playing with you, Adam."

"Then stop acting like a little bitch."

He wouldn't let up and eventually I'd had enough. I turned and got right in his face. I could tell that he didn't think I was going to do anything, which got me even more upset, so I just hit him. For a couple seconds he might have been out cold because he dropped and just laid there. *Oh shit!* Even I was surprised. The family stood around Adam as he picked himself up off the ground, but my dad pulled me off to the side to calm me down.

"He's your cousin. Don't be doing that," he said.

"But he wouldn't leave me alone."

"You can't hit him."

"Then what? Just let him keep talking to me?"

"The next time you get upset or feel angry, step aside and do some pushups. I bet you can't even do 20."

I didn't respond. I just dropped and knocked out 40 pushups right there.

My father understood what I was going through. I saw what happened when he got angry and I knew he was on medication. There was a history of mental illness in my family. Everybody has problems and people deal with those problems differently. It's hard to get support from your family or the people in your community when they're dealing with their own problems. There were not many well-balanced people in the environment I grew up in, so most of the time I had to figure things out on my own.

But nobody can do it all alone. Luckily there was this free counseling service in our neighborhood. It's not there anymore, but there used to be an apartment on the 40-side of 10th Street that was strictly used for therapy. It was great because anybody in the neighborhood could go there for help. By the time I was 13 I had gotten into so many fights that my mom made me go, and I'm glad she did. That was the first time I was told that I might have an anxiety disorder. The psychologist I met with was a really good guy and he helped me get control of my temper. He used to take me to the park to play football after we talked and then he'd buy me some food.

I may not have gone looking for trouble, but there were plenty of times when I crossed the line. I could recognize that. Once, when I was outside on the block, these guys started bothering me. I ran inside and got a pair of scissors. I was ready to cut somebody. Thankfully nothing bad happened, but a situation like that made me realize that I had to get control of my emotions. When I found myself wanting to hurt somebody, I had to make sure that I wasn't going to do anything that would land me in jail. You could never back down in my neighborhood, but as I got older I started to learn when not to fight. Things can go wrong very quick, and that's when people get stabbed and shot.

There was one situation that could have gotten real bad. It happened when I started sixth grade at IS-8. I had been at the school a week and didn't know anybody. One day I was running late to class. I walked into the stairwell when these five guys from this Latino gang cornered me. They must have seen me in the hall and followed me. One kid got right up in my face.

I knew who these guys were. They were a little older than me and had some beef with my cousin Wally. I guess they couldn't get to him so they tried to punk me instead.

Class had already started. Nobody else was around. I was stuck in this stairwell and outnumbered. There was no way I'd be able to take them all, but I wasn't just going to stand there and let them kick my ass either. I knew that if I got in a couple shots I might be able to get away.

Smack! I hit the kid in front of me right in the side of his head with everything I had. I didn't even wait to see what happened to him. I took one swing each at the two kids closest to me and just took off running out of the stairwell. I made it to the hallway and rounded the corner but saw they weren't following me. I got away, but I still had to wait and hide out until 5:00 PM before I could go home.

I knew that wouldn't be the end of it. I could have easily gone and got my friends. We could have found some kids who really didn't have anything to live for, but that would mean getting involved in the gang life. I was surrounded by those people and saw them every day, but that lifestyle was something I was never into. You have to protect yourself, but I didn't want to get into trouble and I definitely did not want to go to jail. After I got jumped, the best thing for me to do was to get out of that school. I told my mom what happened and she helped me transfer to 204, which was right down the block and a school where I knew more people.

I never talked to Wally about that incident, and I never crossed paths with those guys again, but that was just another example of what my life was like. It wasn't out of the ordinary and I didn't worry about it. All I cared about was surviving.

Chapter 2

Streetball

"Ron, have you ever considered organized sports?" That's what the principal asked me when I found myself back in his office after another fight. This time he wasn't mad. It felt like he was legitimately trying to help me.

"That might be a good outlet for your aggression," he said.

I wasn't into sports before that. Instead, me and my friends were playing tag, double dutch, skully, catch-one-catch-all, and stickball. We were active and we were outside all day long, but I didn't play basketball until I was eight years old. In my neighborhood, that's pretty late. A lot of kids started playing as soon as they could walk.

The first time I picked up a ball and actually played was with Wally. We went out to the courts on 12th Street and it was immediately clear that I had no idea what I was doing. I kept trying to put the ball through my legs, but I couldn't do it. I wasn't good, but it was fun. Playing that one time made me want to learn and get better.

Pretty soon I wanted to play all the sports. My dad was a Golden Gloves boxer, but he didn't want us to get hit, so he never allowed us in the ring. I saw some of his fights and I think it took its toll on him, so I appreciate him looking out for us. I tried playing football once in middle school, but I hurt my knee when I got tackled in tryouts. I couldn't play basketball for two weeks, so I said "fuck that shit" and quit the team.

I started to get serious about the game when I was about 10. I'd play a lot with my older cousin Butchy, who lived with my grandmother down in Far Rockaway. He'd help me work on my game, but the person who put in the most time with me was my dad. He'd come home from work and take me to the courts on 12th Street, which became my second home. We'd be out there all day long. Sometimes there would be pickup games, but toward the end of the night we'd have the court all to ourselves. We'd play full-court one-on-one until 3:00 in the morning. And he wouldn't just play; he'd play hard. He'd foul me and try to scare me. My dad was like 6'2" and 250 pounds, and he wouldn't go easy on me. When I hit the ground hard, I'd have to pick myself up.

"Finish the play. Don't worry about the foul. There ain't no whistles out here," he'd tell me.

That's how I first learned to play hard and that's what made me tough. I was also having a lot of fun.

Once I started playing basketball I never stopped. I played all day, every day. It's all I wanted to do. I never found a reason not to play and I tried to play everywhere I could. I also never let the weather get between me and basketball. I liked to go out to the courts on 12th Street when it rained really hard because it felt like the court was mine. When it snowed, me and my friend Cedric would shovel off the blacktop and break up the ice. Every once in a while, we'd strip down to our shorts and go play in the snow for 30 cents a game. Once or twice a winter, we'd try to play with no shoes on to see who was tougher and could last longer.

We didn't have any middle school or elementary school teams. What we had was the community. My first official "coach" in Queensbridge was Bob Welch from the Jacob Riis Center. We used to call him "Bob Riis," and he was the one who first taught me how to shoot free throws. He was a white guy with blond hair who became the unofficial commissioner of basketball in the Queensbridge projects.

Everyone in the neighborhood knew that Bob was the glue. We trusted him, and he was one of the guys who really cared about us. Any time something racial went down in the neighborhood, it always made us think of Bob before we said or did anything out of line. People in the neighborhood had the utmost respect for Bob. He was basically untouchable. He helped make the Riis Center the Mecca of basketball in Queens.

They had some great games at the Riis Center. Vern Fleming was from my block. He lived right on the corner of 41st and 10th Street. His niece had a baby with my cousin Aaron. Sean Greene was from the 40-side of Vernon, Nas' block. They both played for the Pacers, and a few years later I went on to play for them, too. It was crazy to have three people from the same neighborhood all play for the same NBA franchise. But as a kid I never thought about becoming a professional. I was just playing to have fun. I dreamed about where I'd play ball in high school more than I ever did about where I'd go to college.

In our neighborhood, everyone wanted to play for St. Rita's Catholic Church, in Long Island City. We all looked up to the older guys on that team and wanted to be just like them. People from the neighborhood told me I should try out, so that's what I did when I was nine or 10. I thought I played well, but when the coaches lined up everyone to announce who made the team, my name wasn't called. That was a bad feeling. I didn't get mad. It just made me want to get better because I knew that I could make that team. Even when I was young, I never got down on myself. I was always confident that I could be a good player if I put in the work. I had to wait an entire year, but I made that team the following season.

St. Rita's was the first time I played organized basketball. Playing on the playground or at the Boys Club was one thing, but playing organized basketball took some getting used to. I was still trying to win, but now we had refs calling fouls and there were a whole bunch of other rules I wasn't used to. There was a shot clock. I'd see kids setting screens and picks. They didn't do that out on the playground.

My friends were always better players than me. I didn't have the skills, partly because I hadn't been playing that long. I couldn't shoot. I couldn't put the ball behind my back. My game was pure heart. I was stronger than the other kids and I could outrun people, but my offensive game was weak. That's why, even at a young age, I had to make sure my defense made up for it. That's what I put my energy into. I always knew that I wanted to compete, but I also knew that I needed to get better.

Paul Meade was our coach at St. Rita's and he played college ball, so he was able to teach me about head fakes, drop steps, and pivots. He made me better, and over the next couple years our team got real tight. Mel Kennedy was another coach who took my game to the next level. He played with Rick Carlisle at Virginia. When we were playing at the Boys Club on 21st Street, he taught me how to get my shot off and how to shoot with my left hand. Each coach was able to teach me something different, so little by little I improved. I'd take what I learned and go to the park so I could work on it. I'd work on my handle. I'd work on my jump shot.

I wasn't super tall as a kid. I did most of my growing later, but I was still tall enough for coaches to stick me in the post. I was stubborn and always tried to stay outside. To be a true big man, I figured I had to be seven feet tall, and I knew I wasn't going to be that big. I knew that I needed other skills. Even when I was young I used to take the ball out to the wing a lot. I wanted to be in control of the game and bring the ball up if the guards weren't available. A lot of times I'd get the rebound and go coast to coast. Even today, I still find myself thinking like that. I've always wanted to take over the game.

So much of my development as a young player had to do with being able to learn from all the different coaches in the community, but kids today don't have that same opportunity. That's one reason why I think New York City basketball is on the decline. Back in the day there used to be all kinds of tournaments and leagues, but you don't see that as much anymore and it hurts the community. Kids don't play basketball like they used to. A lot of places like the Riis Center are gone, as are those father figures in the community like Bob Riis who would help kids any way they could.

The one place the city will never be able to shut down or take away from us is the playground. Streetball provided me with an entirely different type of basketball education. I was always mean on the court, but that's how you had to be if you were from 12th Street. You didn't have a choice because nobody gives you anything on the playground. There were no fouls. You had to play through everything. You couldn't just be out there bullshitting. Nobody was having that. If you were one of those guys, they just wouldn't let you play.

There is no age limit on the playground. Anyone can show up and play, so I was going up against grown men. I didn't give an inch. To get respect, you had to go all in. If not, people would start calling you soft, and that's the worst thing you could be. There was no way in the world anybody was going to call me soft. It was survival of the fittest. Everybody went hard and laid it all out on the line because nobody wanted to go home with a loss. Winning was all you had out there, and I learned early on that one of the keys to winning was defense. Even at a young age, my defense was crazy. Locking people up has always been something I've enjoyed and took pride in doing. My father told me that he was the same way. He never considered himself the best player, but he would take it personally if somebody scored on him. He felt like he had failed. Some of that must have rubbed off on me because I didn't ever want anybody to score on me.

The courts on 12th Street were the closest to my apartment and had some of the best games, but we played all over. Sometimes we'd play in Baby Park under the 59th Street Bridge. There were guys coming from every other block to play down there because the games were amazing. There was DS Park in Ravenswood. Maybe we'd go to 45th Row, right on Vernon Boulevard toward the Midtown Tunnel. They had good games over there, but those were some scary walks because we never knew what kind of crackheads or prostitutes we'd run into. Sometimes I'd go down to those courts just to shoot and get away from everything.

I also learned that I had to eat well if I wanted to have enough energy to be outside playing ball all day. But one of the most difficult things for me growing up was getting enough food to eat. We'd have some good meals as a family on Thanksgiving and other holidays, but it was really hard to eat well all the time. We never had a lot of vegetables. Back in the day, everything was cooked in lard, and that made me feel sluggish. It was the same with all the fried chicken we used to eat. Sometimes my dad was able to buy food on credit. He used to work as a delivery man and had relationships with stores that would give us some food to help us out. That always came in handy. While he was working at the hospital, we could sometimes go to the cafeteria and get a burger. My dad always told me to eat fruit, so I used to go to the store and buy oranges. I'd bring those with me to the courts and eat them when I was playing. I tried to make them last as long as possible by peeling back the fiber layer and eating each piece one at a time.

I wasn't inside long enough to watch much television so I didn't follow pro basketball at all at that time. One of my first basketball memories was seeing B.J. Armstrong hit a shot from the corner for the Chicago Bulls during the playoffs. I must have been eight or nine years old. That was the first time I ever saw anybody score in a game on TV, and that's what made me a Bulls fan. Not Michael Jordan or Scottie Pippen, but B.J. Armstrong. It was so cool to see guys playing basketball on TV. I didn't even know who B.J. was at the time. I only figured that out later when I was playing those NBA video games. Whenever we played video games, I was always the Bulls. I remembered that the guy I saw hit the shot was No. 10, so that's how I learned it was B.J. Armstrong.

B.J. was always my favorite player, but I still didn't like to watch much basketball. I liked to play. All the people I modeled my game after were from the streets. It's crazy to think about how many talented basketball players were in our neighborhood. The one player everyone asks me about is Lloyd Newton. He was a legendary player from Queens who passed away much too early. This is a crazy story. He was playing in a YMCA tournament up in Niagara Falls at the Boys and Girls Club when a brawl broke out and Lloyd was killed by a table leg that went through his chest. He was dead before he got to the hospital. A lot of people think I was there, but I was only 11 at the time. A bunch of us were back in Queens waiting for those guys to come back with a win.

Everyone looked up to Lloyd. He was a real baller. I remember watching him play on 10th Street and over at the Riis, but I never got the chance to play with him because he was seven years older than me. After Lloyd died, the games in Queensbridge started to change. The intensity went up and it felt like people were playing for Lloyd.

Kenny Eato was a guy I owe a lot to. Not only was he a really good player, but he acted like a pro. He was supposed to play in the McDonald's All-American game and then go play for the University of Oklahoma, but he lost his scholarship when he got involved with drugs and was shot. I played with him in leagues after he got out of jail, and he taught me a lot about being a professional. There was also Desheen Cook, who went to school in Queens. Dwayne Edwards played with me at La Salle and ended up getting a scholarship to James Madison. Then there's my boy Skins, who also took me under his wing. I had Top Boogie, Super Ed, and Nice from the hood. There are so many people who I have to pay homage to. They took time to play with me on the court and helped me get better by making it tough for me to score.

All those guys were great basketball players, but the one everyone on the street really idolized was Mike Chatfield. He was only a year older than me, but he had been playing much longer. He was a tough point guard who could shoot, and he had that Derek Fisher–type of heart that you can't teach. It was like he was ready to fight every time he stepped onto the court, but he was also an extremely intelligent basketball player. I was 13 years old when I played one-on-one with him in the Riis Center and I think he beat me 32–2. I tried everything but nothing worked. After that game, I told myself that I had to get better.

Mike Chatfield was a real dude. He wasn't only well respected on the basketball court; he was respected in the street by the hustlers. He was one of the best players in the city at 15, but he ended up going to jail that same year. I think Mike Chatfield might have played a little after he got out of jail, but he got involved in the street life. He tried to make a comeback but he was in and out of trouble. He just couldn't let that lifestyle go. He was shot and killed during a drug deal gone wrong in 2009. It's a shame, because he's another guy who could have gone on to play in the NBA. I still tell people today that he's the best basketball player I've ever played against. There was nobody like him. I'm just thankful my life didn't follow down the same path.

Chapter 3

Life on Fire

The year I turned 13 was a tough one for me, and it started with a fire in our apartment.

I was with my dad at the time. I had gone out with him to run errands and get groceries. On the way home, we could see smoke in the distance. When we made it to our street, we could see that the smoke was coming from our building. Everyone had cleared out and was standing on the sidewalk.

My stomach sank. I knew it was our apartment before anybody on the street told us. I saw people coming up to my dad to explain what happened. I felt scared for my family. *Was anybody inside? Is anybody hurt?* I tried to remember where everyone was supposed to be that day.

Apparently our downstairs neighbor had run back into our apartment because he thought my little brother Khalik was still inside. Luckily, Khalik had gotten out, but my neighbor was badly burned.

We lost almost everything we had. The apartment was destroyed and our cat died in the fire, but things could have been so much worse.

If I had to guess how the fire got started, I would say it had something to do with the loose wire that was poking out of the wall in our bedroom. My parents worked hard but we didn't always have money to take care of the apartment. Usually the housing authority would fix those issues, but they couldn't repair that one wire for whatever reason, so we just left it the way it was. The way that we kept playing around with that thing, we probably fucked it up even more.

Immediately after the fire, our family was scattered all over the place trying to figure out where we would live. It wasn't long before housing found us a new apartment on the 40-side of Charles Street. The apartment that burned down was a three-bedroom, so there was never a lot of room considering on any given day we had about 15 people living in there. The new apartment that housing found for us was only a one-bedroom. I was with my sisters and my mom when we walked into that one-bedroom apartment for the first time. Nobody said anything. We knew it was going to be small, but actually seeing it was shocking. It didn't seem like we'd ever be able to fit in there.

"It's just temporary." That's what my mom kept saying. She had a way of keeping things positive and making us feel like everything was going to be okay, but at first it was tough. We brought in a bunch of mattresses and laid them out across the floor. Everyone was on top of each other, so we had to make sure to take quick showers. We did this for an entire summer.

Before the fire we were always trying to move out of that old apartment and find a place with more room. None of us ever thought we would actually move to a smaller apartment. But as it turned out, we had so much fun in that one-bedroom.

There were no issues and we did everything together as a family. Everyone was always playing games. We were tight. I think that's why even today I always like to have a lot of people around the house.

After that summer, the city found us a five-bedroom apartment back on 10th Street but things didn't get any easier. That same year my parents finally decided to end their marriage. I found out late one night. It was about 10:30 PM when I got home from the courts on 12th Street. The lights were off in the house. That was strange, because the lights were never off. It gave me a bad feeling.

Daniel, Isaiah, and Khalik were all in the bedroom watching TV. I had picked up a bunch of candy bars and cookies that day and dumped them all out on the bed. I always tried to bring junk food home for them since we never had any at the house.

I saw my dad standing in the hall. He motioned me over with a nod. He had this sad look on his face so I didn't ask what was up. I left my brothers with the candy and followed him into the kitchen. We both sat down at the table when he just flat-out said, "Me and your mom aren't going to make it."

"What?" I knew what he was saying, I just didn't want it to be true.

"We're getting divorced."

I still couldn't believe what I was hearing.

"What can I do?"

"You know things haven't been good. You've seen what's been going on here. It's for the best. You know that, Ron."

I probably asked if there was anything I could do four or five more times. I wanted to fix it. I wanted to make things right, but I couldn't. As hard as it was to watch my parents fight, it was even harder to think of them being apart. I had a ton of questions. *Do we have to move? Would the family get split up? Am I still going to see you? What about my brothers and sisters?*

My dad must have read my mind because he answered before I could even ask one.

"All of you are gonna stay here with your mom. You're not going anywhere."

"And you?"

"I'm moving out, but I'm still gonna be around every day. I'll come by the house. We'll play ball. I just won't be living here. Everything else will be exactly the same."

"Where are you going?"

He shook his head. "I don't know yet, but we'll make it work."

The divorce definitely released emotions in me that I wasn't used to. I was angry a lot as a kid, but this was different. I had never felt that way before. I felt like I was sick, but there was nothing I could do to make myself feel any better.

Even though my parents weren't together, I still saw my dad every single day just like he said. He kept his promise and he made it work. He lived nearby and was always there for me. We kept playing basketball together and he also made sure to visit his grandkids. All the kids in the house loved it when he came by. They used to sing to him so he would give them candy. My dad has done some fucked-up shit, but he's still my dad.

Wally was always hanging out down the street so my mom told me that I was the man of the house now. I tried to help out any way possible and even bought some food home when I could. Holidays and birthdays were always important to my mom. Thanksgiving and Christmas were big at the house, but so was Easter. Mom used to tape money to the Easter eggs and hide them around the house for all the kids to find. It's something we all did as a family. Even though Dad was not living with us anymore, Mom held it down. She always made sure we had clothes and food. She was the one.

Chapter 4

Just Say No

I grew up in the middle of the crack epidemic. Queensbridge was a hotbed for drugs because we were right next to the bridge. People would come from out of town to sell drugs in our neighborhood, and the local dealers didn't appreciate people from outside the neighborhood stealing their business. That was the reason behind a lot of the gun wars.

Drugs were so easily accessible. Every day I was around the hustle, so it was easy to get sucked into that life. A lot of my really good friends did, like Havoc's brother, Killa Black. Havoc always mentions him in his records. It happens fast. Everybody had different family members or friends who did stuff in the streets and I was no exception. My brother Wally would later get locked up for 10 years. My cousins Adam and Aaron used to sell a little dope over on 12th Street. Adam was the younger brother, but he was still six years older than me.

If I wasn't playing basketball, I'd be at my cousins' house. They lived a block away in an apartment right next to Mobb

41

Deep and always had food in their fridge. We'd watch karate movies and play Nintendo, but when I was over there I'd also see them cooking crack on the stove. As a kid, I didn't even know what they were doing. I didn't know it was illegal. I didn't know you could go to jail for that shit.

A lot of times I'd tag along with Aaron when he went over to 12th Street, just to hang out on the block. By the time I was 13, I knew what he was doing. I knew he was selling dope, but that's what everyone did. It was normal. I even got used to the routine. I saw how things went down. I knew how they'd make the exchange. I could spot the people who were there to buy.

I could also spot trouble. One day I saw it before Aaron did. It was a cop. The guy was black and he was wearing street clothes, but he was a cop. I could tell.

"Aaron!"

He looked at me over his shoulder and must have seen the look in my eyes because he took off sprinting. There were about 10 of us on the corner and everyone ran in different directions, but that cop was headed right for Aaron. I don't know if I wanted to help him or if I didn't want to leave him behind, but I followed after Aaron. I quickly caught up and blew right past him. I rounded the corner and headed for Aaron's building.

He shouted, "Ron! No!" He knew we shouldn't go back to the apartment, but I wasn't thinking straight and I just kept running. Aaron followed. So did the cop who was about a hundred feet behind us when we busted through the entrance and took the stairs two at a time.

I made it to the apartment first. I opened the door and waited. It felt like forever before Aaron got there. I could hear the cop coming up the stairs behind him. When Aaron made it inside, I slammed the door and locked it. Adam was sitting on the couch playing video games. He jumped up and said, "What the hell?"

I didn't answer him. Shit had just got real. I was scared. I did not want to go to jail. I also did not want my parents to find out I'd been out on the corner. They would whoop me if I got in trouble for anything involving drugs. I always figured that if I wasn't selling I couldn't get into trouble, but that clearly wasn't the case.

BANG, BANG, BANG! Those weren't knocks. The cop was fucking pounding on the door.

"Open the fuck up!" he yelled.

I flipped. This cop was going to bust down the door any second and take us all to jail. I saw some baggies and vials sitting on the kitchen counter by the stove, so I grabbed them and sprinted to the bathroom.

Aaron knew what I was doing and was right on my heels. I was ready to dump all of it in the toilet and flush it, but he grabbed my hand and stopped me.

"I'm not going to jail," I told him.

"Nobody's going to jail," he said.

BANG, BANG, BANG!

"If he could come in, he'd be inside already," Aaron tried to assure me. "He needs a warrant. If we don't open the door, we're straight."

I relaxed a little, but I wasn't going to hand over the drugs to Aaron just yet. If that cop came into the apartment, I was throwing that shit out the window. I didn't care. After about five long minutes, the cop finally left. I didn't flush the drugs. I felt stupid, but I was starting to realize how easy it was to get caught up in the hustle.

That cop could have been some corrupt police officer looking for guns and drugs. You never knew what kind of cop you were dealing with back then. There's a big difference between a police officer and a criminal with a badge. We had both in our neighborhood. There were a few black cops, but most of them were white. There was one white officer we called Robocop who would shake you down, mostly looking for drugs. I heard he got shot, so he might have passed away.

For the most part, my relationship with the police growing up was pretty good. I was always taught to call them when something went wrong, so they could come to take care of the bad guys and make sure everything was okay. Sometimes the police officers showed up at the basketball courts when we were out there playing. They'd actually put down their guns and play ball with us.

I wish I could say that being chased scared me straight, but it didn't. I was only 13, but I could see that people made good money selling drugs. Everybody was doing it and I wanted to make some of that money. I asked my cousins and they walked me through the process of how to cook crack. First, I had to cut up a batch. It took me a while to get it right. Once it was cut, I had to put the rocks in these little vials. I had no idea where they came from, but there were thousands of those vials all over the streets.

We wrapped up the vials in a paper bag and my cousins sent me outside to meet someone on the corner. All I had to do was hand that person the bag and get the money from them. It sounded so simple, but I was on edge the entire way down the stairs. As soon as I stepped foot outside, my anxiety level went through the roof.

"Hey, little man. Over here."

There was a big burly guy with a beard standing on the corner, and he was talking to me. I was so scared that I just stood there.

"You got something for me?" he asked.

I looked around and was conspicuous as hell as I handed over the paper bag. I think the guy even laughed. That made me more nervous so I just ran back into the building. I didn't even take the money. I was so scared that I was going to get arrested and go to jail that I didn't want any part of that money exchange. When I got back up to the apartment my cousins were a little upset at first, but they couldn't help but laugh. That was the first and last time I ever tried to sell drugs. I was not cut out for that life.

When my parents found out that Aaron and Adam were selling drugs, they told me to stop hanging out with them immediately. From then on, I always tried to stay out of trouble. I was in the mix, but I didn't even smoke weed until I got older. Whenever somebody would offer me drugs or ask me to do something illegal, I never got involved. Nobody was gonna punk me into anything, because I wasn't trying to get into any trouble.

Most of my friends didn't have both parents living in the same house. I'd say like 95 percent of them didn't know who their dad was. But in our neighborhood, if your father wasn't in your life then the streets raised you. When that happened, it was very easy to make bad decisions and be led in the wrong direction. That's why family is so important. They are there to steer you in the right direction. I was lucky enough to grow up with both of my parents. They taught me a lot about respect and it's because of them that I stayed out of trouble. I always knew that I didn't want to go to jail, but I still feared a whooping more than anything.

As I got older, a lot of people in the neighborhood started looking out for me. Every once in a while, I'd run into these OGs who would tell me to stay focused. They could have tried to get me to follow in their footsteps, but instead they'd always tell me to stay on the court. They gave me a little bit of extra motivation and encouragement to keep at it.

Meanwhile, I'd see more and more kids getting into trouble. Kids were getting locked up or worse. We'd always hear stories about how this guy could have been this or that guy could have been that. I knew I wanted to do something with my life. I knew I didn't want to go down that same path. That's why I questioned every decision I made.

Chapter 5

A Way Out

In the hood you either rap, sell drugs, or play ball.

I couldn't rap. Selling drugs didn't work out. But I was starting to get good at ball. That's what I loved most. And after my parents' divorce, I had a lot of built-up anger and frustration that I was able to get out on the basketball court. No matter how difficult things were at school or at home, I could always play basketball. That's where I was in my element and the most comfortable. Sometimes basketball felt like the only thing in my life that I could control.

All of that anger and aggression helped me when playing on the block, but sometimes it hurt me when playing in an organized league. The absolute worst was when my team lost. I wasn't able to deal with losing. I just hated it so much. I was always getting into trouble after games we lost. I'd throw stuff, blame everyone else, and curse out my teammates.

There was one Catholic Youth Organization game in eighth grade that I'll always remember. We were playing against St.

Joe's at their small shoebox of a gym. They were pretty good. We were better. We should have been winning, but we were down. I wasn't playing well. Shots weren't falling, but I wasn't getting any calls either. I was bigger than a lot of the guys on the court, so I'd get hit hard every time I went to the basket but it wouldn't get called. That's fine and all, but don't call me for touch fouls down at the other end of the court when I'm playing defense. That's what was happening and I was getting heated.

With a couple minutes left, the point guard from St. Joe's missed a three. I was at the foul line when the shot went up, but I went after the ball and grabbed the rebound. We now had a chance to tie the game and I was going to take over. I took the ball, found my opening, and drove to the basket. I had a clear path, but some kid came out of nowhere and smacked my arm. I missed the shot. I went after the rebound, but the St. Joe's point guard got there first. I had been chasing that kid around all day. We must have gotten tangled up because he went down and the whistle blew. I looked up and the ref was looking right at me. He called a foul on me for tripping.

"No fucking way!" I screamed.

I was ready to get up in this guy's face. My teammates must have seen the look in my eye because they were out on the court, trying to drag me back to the bench. Honestly, I don't even know what was going through my mind. I wasn't thinking. I was just reacting. I grabbed one of the folding chairs and threw it at the ref. I didn't come close to hitting him, but the whole place went nuts. Both benches cleared. All hell broke loose. People were being held back. It felt like a wrestling match. I must have been trying to break away and go after the ref because my teammates were holding my arms tight and trying to push me toward the back of the gym.

That's when Artie Cox approached me. Artie was a coach for St. Joe's, though he wasn't coaching this game. He was in the stands and saw the whole thing.

"Ron, come take a walk," he said.

He put an arm around my shoulder and took me down the stairs and into a bathroom that I didn't even know was there. It was creepy and damp.

"What are you doing?" he asked me.

"I keep getting fouled!"

"Ron, who cares? So you're not getting calls. Life goes on. Did you know the ref you just threw a chair at is an off-duty cop?"

Shit. I didn't know that. I started to worry. *Will they arrest me now?*

"You can't be doing things like that."

Artie was mad but he was talking to me like a person. He wasn't like a teacher or a principal who'd just yell or try to punish me.

"What did you think was going to happen? How is throwing a chair going to help you? It's a long season. You're going to see this ref again. Do you think he's going to give you any calls now?"

I didn't have any answers for him. What he was saying made sense. I knew I was being stupid so I didn't try to defend my actions.

"You're a good kid, but if you keep acting like this you won't be able to play. And then what are you gonna do? You don't want to be another thug on the street who winds up in jail."

"I know."

"Smarten up."

He patted me on the shoulder and walked back up the stairs.

I was embarrassed, standing there alone in that bathroom. I don't really know what it was about Artie, but he got through to me that day.

Artie was also the coach of an AAU team called Brooklyn/Queens Express—a name he came up with after joining forces with the coach of St. Anne's in Brooklyn and wearing out his car driving back and forth on the expressway. He took down my number that day, and I started playing with BQE. Artie was the coach who would turn my life around. He was the one who told me how good I could be if I could just learn how to calm down. Playing for Artie, I learned more about team basketball. He was exactly the type of coach I needed at the time, just like Phil Jackson would be many years later in Los Angeles.

As I got better I started to believe what he was saying. My family recognized the change in me, too. They looked out for me. The practices were always in Brooklyn at the Boys Club in Fort Greene. When I wasn't able to take the train, my cousin Adam would drive me all the way there early on Saturday mornings.

Brooklyn/Queens Express started out small, but we got bigger and we got better—a lot better. One of the players who started at the same time as me was a kid named Lamar Odom. We didn't cross paths on the playground often, but I knew who he was. The first time I ever saw Lamar was when I was 11. We played with each other at DS Park in Ravenswood. I remember that he was shorter than me then. The next summer I saw him and he was five inches taller than me. He grew that fast in one year. Now we were in eighth grade and Lamar could do everything. He was so talented.

Rounding out the BQE team was a great point guard named Erick Barkley and also a kid named Reggie Jessie. Reggie was someone I had been hearing about forever, but I had never met or played against him, even though he lived over on Nas' block on the 40-side. He was a soft-spoken kid who kept to himself, but he had talent. He was tall but he could handle like a guard. As a team, we all came together quickly and started playing well.

Playing for BQE also gave me my first chance to travel outside of New York City. The first tournament we traveled to was just down the road in New Jersey, but I was still excited. It was an experience and I was so happy for the chance to compete. However, I was still having a hard time controlling my temper; old habits die hard. During one tournament, I lost it when the referee didn't call a foul so I kicked the bleachers and sprained my ankle. I couldn't finish the game. Our assistant coach Kenny Pretlow screamed and told me that I was about to ruin everything that I had worked for. He used a lot of curse words and he was loud. That hit home. I knew I had to change.

Brooklyn/Queens Express was owned by a much bigger team called Riverside Church. Riverside traveled everywhere and were not only one of the best AAU teams in the city, they were one of the best in the country. People used to joke that BQE was the farm team for Riverside, which wasn't far from the truth. Riverside was owned by Mr. Ernest Lorch and he ran the program like a pro team. He probably could have been a good NBA general manager. The first time I met Mr. Lorch was when I was playing for Brooklyn/Queens and we were giving his team hell during a scrimmage. I'd play so hard during those games.

Being an eighth-grader meant it was time to think about where I wanted to play high school ball. The junior high I was at, 204, went up to the ninth grade, but they didn't play against any other high schools, so that wasn't a good option for me. In the meantime, there was a group of us who began to emerge as really good ballplayers in the neighborhood. Paul Meade's son Jave was one, and Mike Chatfield's brother Eric was another. I had met Eric when I was younger and we both played in the local summer tournaments back in Queensbridge. We quickly got used to playing with each other, and neither of us was selfish. For a while we talked about waiting for Mike Chatfield to get out of jail and all going to high school together at Long Island City. We would've had a squad, but Mike didn't come home until I was already in college. It wasn't meant to be, but that team would have been awesome.

Artie was the freshman coach at McClancy High. I liked playing for him because I felt like he got the best out of me. Even at that age I could tell that he was looking out for me. He had taken me to a couple games at McClancy and I liked the school. It was in Queens so I could stay in my borough. I made up my mind to go there. I was committed, but one month before school started I learned there was a problem.

My phone rang one night. It was Artie. I could tell that something was wrong just by the sound of his voice. It turned out that I couldn't get into McClancy because of my grades. I would have to take summer school classes, but it was August and summer classes were all over. School was scheduled to start in a month, but now I didn't have one to go to. My basketball career was about to end before it got started.

Chapter 6

Made in Manhattan

Thankfully, Tyrone Greene stepped up.

Tyrone was an old street coach and referee from the neighborhood who was always around to help the kids. He worked mostly in the Astoria projects, but he'd come down to Long Island City to find talent. When I was younger I used to play for Tyrone in the Police Athletic League.

By mid-August I still didn't know where I was going to school, or if I could even get into a high school that late in the year. That's when I got a phone call from Tyrone completely out of the blue.

"What do you think about going to private school?" he asked.

"Can I do that?"

"If you're interested."

"Whatever I need to do, I'll do it."

"You don't need to do anything. We can get you in if you want to go."

"Absolutely!"

"It's going to be a lot different. Are you okay with that?"

"Wait, what school are we talking about?" I asked, but it really didn't matter. I didn't care. He could have said any school and I would have been grateful to go.

"What do you think about La Salle Academy?"

La Salle was a private school in Manhattan. Tyrone had a connection to its program and its head coach, Bill Aberer. I knew the history of those private schools. Some of the best players in the city played at private schools. La Salle had an All-American named Shammgod Wells. He had just finished his sophomore year, but he was already an amazing basketball player who was getting a lot of attention nationally. I was well aware that this private school thing might be good for my career, and the chance to play with someone like Shammgod was a great opportunity. I've always been excited to try new things, and I wanted a fresh start, so when I got the chance to go to La Salle, I jumped at it.

"Sign me up," I told Tyrone.

Tyrone had gotten a lot of kids from the Queens area into La Salle, including Eric Chatfield, who had already enrolled. I also knew Dwayne Edwards, who was a junior at La Salle. He grew up in Queensbridge on the 41st side of Vernon. There were a lot of kids on that team whom I had known or played against before in CYO.

But there was still one big problem. Tyrone and Bill Aberer were able to get me into La Salle, but it was August and they were out of scholarship money. I couldn't pay my way through private school. Aberer called up Artie Cox, who then spoke with Mr. Lorch. Luckily, they were able to pay for me to go to La Salle through the tuition assistance program Mr. Lorch had set up at Riverside Church.

I was finally able to relax. With a couple weeks before the start of the school year, I played as much ball as possible. One night, practice with BQE and Riverside ran late. I was exhausted and not looking forward to that long train ride home from Brooklyn. I packed up my bag and wanted to get out of there quick when Mr. Lorch came up to me.

"How are you doing on clothes?" he asked.

"I'm cool."

I had no idea what he was talking about.

"You'll have to start wearing a coat and tie to school now."

Shit. I had completely forgotten about that because of all the drama around just trying to get into school. I didn't have any time to think about what I was going to wear when I got there. I couldn't just show up in my street clothes. There was a dress code at La Salle and I didn't have any of the clothes that would pass it.

"I can probably borrow something from my dad," I told him.

Mr. Lorch laughed and said, "Come with me tonight. I'll drop you at home after."

He took me to a department store nearby and helped me pick out everything I needed. I got a blazer, a tie, shoes, slacks—all that stuff. I never had to wear anything like that before. It was all so different, but I was excited.

All I had to do then was figure out how to get to school. I ended up taking the Q train from the 21st Street train station to 42nd Street and then changed over to the F train and took that to 2nd Avenue. It was about a 45-minute trip each way. Even if I didn't have a game or practice at night, I wouldn't get home until 6:30 PM. I didn't care. I loved that ride home on the train. It was such a good feeling to spend all day at a Catholic school in the city and then come back home to the projects at night.

La Salle was an eye-opening experience. It was so much different from the public schools in Queens. Kids from all over the world attended La Salle, so I definitely experienced some culture shock. There were a lot of Puerto Ricans and Dominicans at La Salle. Lots of Latinos. I also found out right away that the schoolwork there was hard. I don't remember my math teacher's name, but on the second day she stood at the front of the class and said, "Put your books away, we're going to have a little quiz."

I looked to the kid next to me and asked, "What? She didn't say anything about this yesterday." The kid just shrugged and didn't seem to care, but I was panicking when the teacher passed out those test papers. Math was one of my better subjects, but I didn't know how to answer any of the questions on this test. Not one. I tried as best as I could but I was completely lost.

When I showed up for class the next day, I was hoping the teacher wouldn't pass those tests back, but that was the first thing she did. I sat there and watched all the kids around me get A's and B's. That made it so much worse. I had never felt that nervous in school before. She finally put my paper facedown on my desk. For a second I wondered if maybe I was making a big deal out of nothing, but then she said, "Ron, see me after class." I knew it wasn't good. I flipped over the paper and saw "38" and "F" written out in red. I hid the paper inside my book. I didn't want anybody else to see it. It was only the first week and I already felt like I didn't belong.

Before I knew it, I was failing all of my classes. The teachers weren't going to give me passing grades just because I played basketball. I was putting in the effort, but I didn't know what I was doing. I was discouraged, but I had to keep pushing myself. The classes were the toughest thing about La Salle, but it was a blessing in disguise because it made me work harder. I definitely did not want to fail my way off the basketball team.

When it came to playing ball, I had a reputation around New York City. I was only 13 going on 14, but I was known for playing tough defense. I was used to being the man when I played CYO, but when I got to high school, everybody was good. It's like that every step of the way. You have to change and adapt at every level or you won't be able to compete.

I went into La Salle expecting to play freshman ball. I actually wanted to play on the freshman team, because I didn't think I was good enough to make the varsity. When you play freshman ball, you get a chance to compete, which is better than sitting on the bench for the varsity. That's what everyone did at that time in the city. I don't know of any freshman from my era who played on the varsity. Even Lamar played on his freshman team at Christ the King. New York City basketball was tough. It's not the same now, but back then it was just grimy and hard-nosed basketball. We had players like Stephon Marbury and Felipe Lopez, who were the best in the country.

My freshman season got off to a rough start. Ray Polanco was my coach. He was a former cop and was really hard on us. The La Salle practices were way more structured than I was used to. At first it was difficult for me to get to practice on time. I just wasn't used to the schedule or the area. The first time I showed up late, Coach P yelled at me in front of the whole team. To make it worse, he wouldn't let me practice.

I was mad. I couldn't believe that he was actually going to sit me. My father was mad, too. I think he might have said something to Coach P, but he wouldn't cave or give in. He sat me for a couple games and I made sure to get to practice on time.

Sitting on the bench was bad, but things got so much worse after I got into a fight at school. I don't remember exactly what happened because I didn't think it was that big of a deal at the time. I do remember getting called to the office and learning they were thinking about kicking me out of school. *Whoa! Hang on!* They didn't care who I was—they were not having that at La Salle. I got lucky and they cut me a break. They didn't kick me out but they made it clear I would be gone if there was another incident. I wasn't walking away with any slap on the wrist either. They suspended me for 13 games. That was half the damn season. I thought that punishment was harsh, but it was better than being kicked out of school.

That was the wake-up call that I needed. Basketball was everything to me. I wanted to win. I hurt the team by not playing. They lost almost every game during my suspension. It felt like I had really fucked up. It was an awful feeling and one that I would experience again years later after the Malice at the Palace.

Since I couldn't even practice with the team during the suspension, I worked on getting my grades up. I stayed after school to get help from my teachers when I needed it. If not, I made sure to come home right after school and do my homework. I put in the effort and soon I went from getting F's and D's to C's and B's. Sometimes I even got an A. The suspension gave me a lot of time to reflect. I knew how easily I could have lost that opportunity. If I got kicked out of school and couldn't play basketball, what was I going to do? When I came back to the team, I was a more focused and serious player.

That didn't mean I lost the fire. Coach Polonco was one of the first coaches who purposefully tried to get me riled up. When we were playing against All Hallows later in the year, he wanted to use my anger as motivation. We fell behind early and were down big at halftime. He came barging into the locker room and started screaming. It took me a little while to realize that he was screaming at me.

"Why is this team kicking your ass? I thought you were this tough kid from Long Island City."

He was staring right at me. I didn't say anything back, but I was getting mad. Coach P later told me I was rocking in my seat and he thought I was borderline crazy, but that didn't stop him from laying into me.

"You ain't that good. You're all hype."

I needed to prove him wrong so I went out there in the second half like a man possessed. I scored something like 21 points in the second half and helped us come back to win by 10. After the game, I went right up to Coach P and asked, "Am I good now, Coach?"

He laughed. "Yeah, Ron. You're pretty good."

That was the first time someone had told me that my intensity was both a blessing and a curse. I'd be hearing that for the rest of my career.

As my freshman season wound down, I started practicing more with the varsity. It was crazy hard to go through two intense practices back to back, but I was pretty tough so I could hang. Playing with the varsity helped me when I went back and played with the freshman team. I found myself reacting more quickly and moving better on the court. I was always the first one to the ball and that helped build my confidence.

I joined the varsity when the freshman season ended. I only played about five or seven minutes a game, but it was a big jump. My first game was against Mount Saint Michael's. They had an All-American named Jarrett Lockhart, who went on to play at Pitt. I had five points, which was rare because I had trouble scoring at the varsity level. Those guys were big. I was barely six feet tall going into freshman year and I still couldn't dunk. I never had hops like that. I was not super athletic so I always had to play smart.

The coaches put in the time and made us all better players. Bill Aberer became like a father figure to me. He was the head basketball coach and was also the computer teacher. He looked out for the players. He made sure we did well in school and stressed the importance of making good life decisions. I was definitely trouble at that time, but he steered me in the right direction and that's what helped me get through some of those tough times. He knew I needed that attention. Whenever I got into trouble, he was the first one to call me into the office. He spoke with this demanding voice and I always found myself trying hard not to let him down.

Our assistant coach, Irv Valentino, also had a major impact on my life. Mr. Valentino coached the Varsity B team, which was like a step up from the JV. He did some coaching at the Five-Star Basketball Camp during the summers. He was a funny guy and, even though he was only 5'2", Mr. Valentino was one man that you did not cross. He was a martial artist, so if you got on his bad side he could probably kill you. That man could put the fear of God in our hearts. He was intense as hell and had this dark side, but we respected and loved him. Looking back, what I respected most about Mr. Valentino was that he held me accountable for my actions. He never kissed my ass and he always kept it 100. At the same time, he would acknowledge you when you did something right. We could have a really good time with him, but he made sure we did the right thing.

As much as I loved my coaches at La Salle, they never gave me anything. I had to earn everything I got, and that's what I did sophomore year when I became a starter. That wasn't easy, considering we had two seven-footers on the team in Gregory Springfield and Karim Shabazz, but I still started at the four. Karim was one of the best sophomores in the city, and he'd later play at Providence College and Florida State. I hadn't seen many guys who were that tall before. Up to that point, I was used to being the tallest guy on the court.

I realized that I had to play a guy like Karim the exact same way I played a guy shorter than me. When we started scrimmaging in practice, it was all about knowing how to use my body. He was taller but I was stronger and had the leverage, so I tried to push him away from the basket and not let him set up where he wanted to on the block. Karim ended up leaving La Salle before senior year, but playing against big boys like that made me better.

I could score when I had to, but I got most of my points because of hustle. I'd get steals and rebounds and turn those into points. I didn't get the ball a lot my sophomore year so I made sure to make an impact with my defense and my rebounding. I'd have games where I'd get like four points and 20 rebounds or no points and 25 rebounds. It didn't matter how big or how good the other guys were, I went into each game with the same mindset. I did the same thing I always did—I just went to get the ball, on both offense and defense. That's what kept me in the starting lineup.

Shammgod was a senior and he was the leader of the team. He set the standard for how we should conduct ourselves and that bar was set high. One time Eric Chatfield and I were walking to practice when we saw that Shammgod was already there running stairs. He'd always be working on his game—before practice, after practice, all the time. When we saw him put in the work, it made us feel like we had to put in the work. That set the tone and helped our team establish a strong work ethic. He made me want to play hard and taught me how to be a leader. I always watched the guys who were the best and tried to push myself so I could be better than them.

The whole team rallied around Shammgod. He got a lot of media attention that year, which was good, because when college coaches came to see him they also got to see me. But for coaches to see me I needed to be on the court. I never liked coming out of the game and did whatever I needed to stay out there.

That's exactly what I did when we played St. Raymond's that year. In the second half I went up to block a shot and got elbowed in the nose. The whistle blew. The game stopped. My head was ringing and then I saw the blood. It was gushing out of my nose. It didn't hurt—it just stunned me. The coaches quickly got me off the court and Coach P took me into the locker room.

"I'm good. Just let me go back in," I said.

"Son, your nose is broken."

"I don't care. I want to finish the game."

My dad came in the back. He took one look at me and said, "Tape him up."

Coach P knew there was no changing my mind, so once my nose stopped bleeding, he gave me one of those clear face masks and I went back in to finish the game. My uniform had blood on it. I had to rip the bloody sleeves off my undershirt so I could go back in the game, but I went in there and grabbed a bunch of rebounds.

It turns out that my nose really was broken and I had to keep wearing the mask. There's still a picture floating around online of me in the mask. Some games I would write things on it and color it with face paint. The media used to get a kick out of that.

That year we had an up-and-down season. We won a lot of games in our division, but we lost to St. Ray's in the playoff semis. They went on to play Lamar Odom and Christ the King in the championship. That was the game when Lamar scored 36 and got the MVP in their victory. Even though he was just a sophomore like me, I remember watching that game and thinking that Lamar was definitely going to the NBA. That game motivated me to push myself and to get better over the summer.

Chapter 7

Ballers

The only way to get better is to keep playing.

If there was a game going on, I was there. Sometimes I'd play three or four games a day. When I wasn't playing for BQE, I sometimes played for another AAU team called Aim High. Eric Chatfield played for Aim High, and we were coached by Kevin Jackson. He was from Queensbridge, and when I was young he would literally chase me and Eric around the projects to make sure we stayed out of trouble. Aim High was run by Kenny Smith's older brother Vincent. He took a lot of the great basketball players from Queens under his wing, including Kenny Anderson back in the day. Vincent became the guru of basketball in Queens, so I enjoyed playing on that team when I could.

I would also play in the adult leagues around the city. The league I really loved was the Rucker League over on 155th Street. When I started playing in the league I was more of a fan. I was on a team with Stephon Marbury and Rafer "Skip

2 My Lou" Alston, who was a legendary streetball player. My first year I mostly watched them, and what I saw those two do on the court was unbelievable. Stephon would pull up from anywhere. I mean, *anywhere*. He could be two or three steps over half court and he'd pull up. And he'd hit those shots consistently. That was unheard of back then. He was an incredible player. As I got older, people in the Rucker started to notice how I would go hard every single play. They hadn't seen that before and that's where I got the nickname "True Warrior."

By the time I was 15, my reputation had grown as a streetball player and I was presented with other opportunities— opportunities to make money and provide for my family. I was at home asleep one night in the summer when the phone woke me up after midnight. We had a lot of people in the house so the phone would sometimes ring late, and people were always trying to call my sisters, but usually never this late. For whatever reason I was the only one who heard it. My brothers slept right through it, so I grabbed the phone before my mom got mad.

"Ron, you up?" It was Mousey, my coach at the Rucker.

"No, why?" I was confused more than anything else, because Mousey had never called my house before.

"I got a game if you're interested."

"A game? Now?"

"You can make some money if you want to."

"What do I gotta do?"

"Just get your ass down to Brooklyn."

Somebody wanted to play me for $500. Mousey put up the money for me. Winner take all. If I won, I'd split it 50-50 with Mousey.

It was the middle of the night, but I didn't have a curfew or anything like that. My mom wasn't worried about me, since she knew I wasn't getting into any trouble or selling drugs. I took a cab to the courts in Brooklyn.

I can't remember who I played against that night, but I won. I ended up playing about four or five more games like that. A lot of times I'd be playing against guys who I knew, but I never lost a money game.

Streetball was fun, but most of the summer was spent playing AAU. By this time, Reggie Jessie, Erick Barley, Lamar, and I were playing for Mr. Lorch on Riverside Church. We also picked up the best player in the city, maybe even the country.

The first time I played against Elton Brand was at the Five-Star Basketball Camp the previous summer. This was way up in the mountains of Pennsylvania. Riverside Church had paid for our team to go. Me and Elton were playing against each other and going at it. I was big, but Elton was bigger. He was 6'9" and he was strong. He would try to knock people around in the post. I wasn't backing down and he wasn't backing down so things got rough. The thing about Elton was that he never got rattled. He was so poised and carried himself like a professional, even though he was still young.

So we're in the middle of this game at Five-Star when I looked down and saw that we both had holes in our shoes. The holes in his looked a little worse than mine, so I was like, "Elton, I need to get you some shoes." We wore the same size so I gave him a pair of mine to wear for the rest of the camp. I can't remember if he took them or not, but we've been close friends ever since.

With Elton on Riverside Church we were now a team with size. Elton was big and could play power forward for us. That freed me up and took a lot of pressure off me. The rest of the team didn't have to do as much.

We spent the whole summer traveling across the country with Riverside Church. Every weekend was a different tournament in a different state. We even went to Italy to play in a tournament, which was a pretty amazing experience. Traveling was fun. I liked getting out of the city and going to all of those different places. We were playing so much basketball that we didn't get to do much else, but I didn't care.

One reason why it was so fun was because we didn't lose. We had a squad and we never took it easy on anyone. We were winning championship games by 60. I'm not lying when I say that our team could have ran in the NBA without any help. The summer before my senior year we finished 69–1. We played everyone and we beat everyone.

Our team was tough. We were mean and we were crazy. Everybody on that team was ready to fight. There were times in practice when me and Elton, or me and Lamar, would get into fistfights. One time Lamar gave me a nasty elbow to the head that opened up a gash. I had to get stitches. Those practices were like NBA practices. It was super competitive and it got me ready for the next level. At one tournament I got into a fight with Elton in the layup line before a game. We won the game and made up after. He was one of my best friends so it was never serious.

College coaches started to follow us around. We'd look up and see Tubby Smith and Rick Pitino sitting in the stands, but I didn't give two fucks. Whenever I was on the court, I was ready to go to war. *Who am I going to fight today?* That's what I was thinking when I stepped out onto the court. I didn't get recruited by a lot of people because of that kind of shit.

When you go to these AAU tournaments, you play three or four games a day for a couple of days in a row. After playing so much ball, it was great just to get back to the hotel so we could eat and watch TV before we got up in the morning and did it all over again. AAU was fun, but it was a grind.

The worst experience I ever had on the road happened when I was at a tournament in Arizona. Elton and I were roommates. We had just got back from buying food and were bullshitting in the hotel room when I decided to call home. We were always gone for so long that I liked to check in on everybody back home whenever I got the chance. My sister Shalice answered and I immediately knew that something was wrong.

"Ron you need to come home," she said.

"What happened?"

I panicked. *Is it my mom? Did someone get shot? Are my brothers and sisters okay?*

Her voice was shaky when she said, "It's Quanisha. She passed away."

I wasn't prepared for that. Quanisha was my two-and-a-half-month-old sister. My mom had just given birth to her in the bedroom of our apartment. My brother Isaiah, who was only 11, cut the umbilical cord. Now Shalice was telling me Quanisha was gone. I couldn't believe it. The whole thing felt unreal.

"How is that possible?"

"She died in her crib. Ron, you need to come home."

I would later learn that she passed away from sudden infant death syndrome (SIDS), but I didn't know what that was at the time.

I couldn't think about the tournament or trying to play basketball. I immediately told Mr. Lorch about Quanisha and he helped arrange a flight for me back home the next day. I didn't get any sleep that night. I stayed up all night watching television. My bags were already packed when the rest of the team left to go to the gym. I hung around a little while longer and took a cab to the airport. It was pouring rain when we took off and the plane hit bad turbulence when we were in the air. It was even raining in New York when we landed.

Being home didn't make things any easier. It was worse. It all felt so much more real. Quanisha hadn't lived very long, but without her there the house felt empty. It didn't matter how many people were inside. I didn't even know what to do with myself. It would be months before I could walk into my mother's room again. Mom had a picture of Quanisha on her bedside table that was hard for me to look at.

The wake was difficult. I held myself together all day, but I couldn't walk in the front door of the funeral home. I just broke down crying on the sidewalk. My sisters had to help me inside, but seeing my sister lying dead in a tiny coffin made my knees weak. My mom and I put one of my basketball trophies in her casket. That was something that had meant a lot to me so I wanted her to have it.

Losing a little sister was tough. That's why I wanted to get her name tattooed on my bicep. Not that I would ever forget her, but it was a reminder and a tribute. I was angry for a long time. I was sad too, but mostly I was mad. My sister's death almost made me feel like I had something to prove.

I don't want to say that I used my sister's death as motivation, but it made that chip on my shoulder a little bit bigger. I carried that chip with me onto the court and never was it bigger than during the summer before my senior year. There were two invitation-only summer camps that the best high school players in the country went to—Nike and Adidas ABCD. I hadn't been invited until that summer, and all of the guys on Riverside decided to attend the Nike camp in Indianapolis.

That was the first time I saw Baron Davis play. Baron was from Los Angeles so we didn't cross paths often. *Who the hell is this little kid?* I thought. But he was so good. Even though he seemed so small, he was always the best player on the court no matter who he was up against. He was fast, he was strong, and he could jump. He had handle and he could shoot. I was blown away, and from that point forward I started following his career. He was one of my favorite players throughout high school. He was talented and he worked hard, so I had a lot of respect for him. Later that summer it was Baron Davis' Team California that gave our Riverside Church team its only loss. Baron's team also had Jason and Jarron Collins, who were two big guys who went on to play at Stanford and then in the NBA. We lost to them early during a tournament in Long Beach but were able to play them again in the championship game and beat them by 20.

After a couple years of playing AAU ball we had seen most of the best players in the country. Now at the Nike camp, all of these All-Americans were in one gym playing in front of college coaches for an entire week. I set out to lock down everyone I guarded. At the end of the camp I went up against 6'10" Chris Burgess from California. He was ranked as a top-five player in the country, but I played him hard and held him to two points. And this was a guy that I heard was thinking of going straight to the NBA. A part of me took that personally, because it felt like the guys from New York were not given the same respect. So when a reporter asked me about the camp, I told him exactly what I was thinking at the time.

"Honestly, I expected better players here," I said. "I hear this kid Burgess is going straight to the NBA, but if he can't post me up I don't see that happening. I locked him up."

A part of me was mad. This had nothing to do with Chris Burgess. This was something bigger that I had noticed for a while. When I'd play against some of the more well-known players my age, I would always lock them up. If a dude was averaging 20 points a game, he was only getting eight or 10 when I guarded him. My defense was definitely better than the other guy's offense, but nobody would notice that. Scoring never interested me, but those other players were getting more attention because they could score. Those were players that I could shut down.

I always prided myself on defense, but I knew I needed to develop an offensive game if I was ever going to be considered one of the best players in the city. More importantly, I was tired of depending on other people to win. To win you had to score, and if I couldn't do it that meant I was relying on everyone else to do all the scoring. I didn't like that feeling. I wanted to have more control over the fate of our team. I had to learn how to score.

I wasn't afraid of the challenge, but it took some work. I would go outside and practice with Rob Johnson at PS-111. Sometimes I'd meet Vincent Smith at a couple gyms in Queens. Even when I was by myself, I would just shoot and shoot and shoot and shoot. I worked on catching and shooting. I practiced some drop steps. I also learned how to shoot with my left hand.

I can actually pinpoint the moment when my offensive game came together and everything started to change for me. It was during the championship game of a men's league in Queens. Anthony Mason from the New York Knicks was on the other team. This was an NBA player known for his toughness and his defense. I never had a chance to play against any NBA players so this was a rare opportunity. I wasn't nervous. I went into that game like I did any other game. I tried to be strong on the court and I didn't back down.

Not only did I try to lock down an NBA player, but I tried to take over the game. I was stepping out of the post and hitting threes. I was driving to the basket. I was always fearless on the court, but not when it came to my offensive game. That game was different. I had no idea how many points I had scored, but I knew that I had a lot.

The game went into overtime. I found the ball in my hands out on the wing with a chance to win. My first thought was to drive to the basket and draw a foul, but my man was playing off me, so I pulled up to take a three and sunk it. Game over. I wouldn't have taken that shot a year earlier. When you knock down big shots, it gives you so much confidence, and confidence is everything. After the game I learned that I dropped 47.

I was only 16, but people were saying that I could go pro. *Oh shit!* For the first time, I actually started to believe that I might be able to play in the NBA.

Chapter 8

The Kings of New York

L a Salle was an all-boys school, and I wasn't even thinking about girls for most of high school, but when I was 15, I met Kimsha on 12th Street. She was sitting on a bench next to the basketball court. Somebody introduced us and I think they might have tried to set us up. She was from the Astoria projects, but I didn't see her again until the following year. It was at the same court, but one bench over. She called me over and then we started talking.

Kimsha quickly became my best friend. When we started dating I thought we'd be together for the rest of our lives. We talked about having a kid right away. I was young, but I wanted a baby. It's hard to say why right now. Maybe it's because my sisters all had babies young. My parents divorced, but they stayed together longer than most. A part of me wanted to succeed where they and so many others in my neighborhood had failed. Find that person who you want to be with and stay with that person for the rest of your life. That was my mentality. I wanted to re-create the love that my parents seemed to have lost. Kimsha and I hadn't even been dating long before we found out she was pregnant in August of 1996.

Everything was different when I went back to school for my senior year. All of a sudden, I had a girlfriend and we were expecting a baby. Also, my grades had improved. When I was a freshman I was basically failing every class. But I kept studying, doing my homework, and going to get help after school. I tried to get better and I did. I was putting in the work and studying hard.

I was also getting more attention as a basketball player. When I first arrived at La Salle as a freshman, I wasn't ranked as a player nationally or even listed as one of the top players in the city. Sophomore year I was starting on the varsity, but I still wasn't ranked. My junior year I was listed as the 110th-best player in the country. I was 55th going into my senior year, and by the end of the season I was 12th.

I didn't do any of it alone. A lot of people helped me out, and someone who made a big difference my senior year was Hank Carter. He was an older man who grew up in Queensbridge. When he was young he was a gangbanger, but he turned his life around and became a successful banker. Even though he had money, he always gave back to the kids in the neighborhood. Somehow he had this deal with Nike, so he'd come down to the community center and drop off hundreds of shoes. That's how I first met him. When I got to high school he hosted a tournament called the Wheelchair Classic. It was big back in the day and had all the best players in the city.

My senior year, Hank reached out and took me into his home. He lived in the city near La Salle and gave me the keys to his house so I was able to go there after school. That got me out of the projects. Sometimes I'd stay over at Kimsha's house, but mostly I was at Hank's. I wasn't permanently moved in or anything, but I was over there a lot. This was also a place where I could eat better food. Hank would always encourage me to go to church with him. He gave me a place to get away from it all and stay focused on my schoolwork. He looked out for me and for that I'm forever grateful.

My grades improved but my main focus that year was winning a championship. I wanted to go out on top. We had a hell of a team, too. It was me, Eric Chatfield, Miguel Caballero, Hector Duprey, Socrates Larrieux, and Von Damien Green. On the court we had set the tone the year before during the McDonald's Classic, a four-team tournament held every year in Erie, Pennsylvania. This was one of the best regular-season tournaments in the country. Patterson Catholic, a school in New Jersey, had future NBA forward Tim Thomas, who was one of the best players in the country. He was a solid 6'9" and was very strong and athletic, so he was a tough matchup. Right before halftime, he dunked over one of our guys. It felt like our guy just stood there and didn't react. I got mad because I thought it made us look weak. At halftime, there was a big whiteboard set up on a stand in the locker room. Coach Aberer was using it to write up plays and I just knocked the thing over. I shouldn't have done that, and I paid the price for acting like that throughout my career, but this time I think it sent a message to our team. We didn't win the game against Patterson Catholic, but we were a different team after that and it carried over into senior year.

At the start of the season I decided that I wasn't going to wash my game jersey or my socks until we lost. I had no idea we were going to go 27–0. I probably would have washed my damn clothes had I known we wouldn't lose a game, but I have no regrets. I'd do it again in a heartbeat if I knew that was the secret to a winning streak. That year we did the impossible. It was a monumental season.

One reason we were so successful was because we did everything as a team. We had all come up in the program together, so we knew each other so well. Senior year we took karate classes together at school. I can't remember if this was something Coach Aberer set up or if it was part of gym class, but those classes helped with our footwork. During the summer we all went down to Five-Star together. When we were back at home, we'd meet up and play together. We might have lived in different parts of the city, but we'd always go hang out at this skating rink over in the Bronx. It was like a club for high school kids. There were girls there so we'd just go to bullshit, but the point was that we were always together.

It wasn't just about winning, either—it was also about how we won. It was about the effort. There was one game where we beat Mount St. Mary's in the Bronx by 20, but it was ugly. A better team would have killed us. I was so mad after that game that I kicked open the door in the locker room and shattered the lock. Coach P looked at me like I was crazy.

"What the hell are you doing?" he asked.

"I'm mad, Coach. We didn't play well."

"We just won by 20."

"We can still do better."

And we did. We finished the regular season undefeated, but that didn't mean anything if we didn't win the city championship. That was the victory I wanted. We had a big semifinal game against Christ the King coming up, so I was going hard during practice. I didn't think the rest of the team was. I was scared we were getting cocky and that the undefeated record was going to guys' heads. So when I saw Miguel Caballero laughing, I got right up in his face.

"Stop fucking around. You're not working hard enough," I told him.

"Fuck you!"

"Fuck me?"

I threw the ball at his head, chased him down, and punched him in the face right there in the gym. We were both big guys and we were throwing blows at each other. The whole team jumped in. Everyone was trying to pull us apart, but it was completely out of control. Our assistant coach, Bruno Cotumaccio, dropped and broke his glasses during the scuffle. When Coach P tried to drag me away, I literally picked him up and moved him out of the way.

Eventually the coaches were able to break it up and get the situation under control. Miguel had a big welt on his head. I don't know if I gave it to him or not, but the coaches got me and Miguel to talk it out. We were cool after that. I was starting to get worried that we might get suspended or not be able to play in the game, but the coaches never reported the fight to the principal. We finished practice like nothing happened, but from that point on everyone played hard. I think that fight is what helped us win that next game.

We beat Christ the King by 10. This was the team that earlier in the year had both Erick Barkley and Lamar Odom, but something happened with Lamar and he transferred to prep school, so he didn't play this time around. I'm not going to lie—that definitely would have been a tougher game if Lamar had been there. We advanced to the finals and beat St. Francis Prep 71–54 to become New York City champions. We were ranked No. 2 in the country and were being considered one of the greatest high school basketball teams in New York City history. That's not bad for a small school on the Lower East Side of Manhattan that played its games in a tiny gym.

Unfortunately our season ended on a sour note when we got bounced from the state tournament in the first round by Long Island Lutheran. They had a big guy named Vassil Evtimov. He was around 6'10" and 250 pounds, and he would go on to play at North Carolina. That team was good, but they were not better than us. It was our own damn fault that we lost that game.

The game was held in Glens Falls, so we had to drive up there and stay overnight. The problem was that the hotel we stayed at had a pool. We brought a boom box down there and spent the whole damn day before the game bullshitting at the pool. Coach Aberer caught us down there and he was furious.

When it was time to play, we were all tired. At one point we were down 20, but nobody had any energy. Long Island went on a 14–0 run in the fourth quarter that put us away. We couldn't run up and down the court, but that was on us. We messed up and can't take it back now.

The season was over and I had to start thinking about college. My goal was to play in the NBA, but by the end of high school I knew that I also wanted to study architecture. I had this vision of building community centers—a lot of them. My interest came from the knowledge that we didn't have what we needed in our neighborhood. I wanted to make the neighborhood better and try to improve the fucked-up situation that we were living in. Whenever I got to leave the city to play basketball, I saw all of these other places that looked so great. Buildings were new and clean. I wanted to build something like that in my own community, but it wasn't until I got older that I realized we couldn't build shit in our community because we didn't really own anything there.

I visited a lot of schools. I looked at Providence, because that's where Shammgod went and he was still a god to me. I also visited Miami of Ohio, because they had an assistant coach, Ray Martin, who was from Queensbridge. But the school I was most interested in was Princeton. If I had the chance, I would have gone there, but I didn't know at the time if I could make it to the NBA from there.

In the end, it came down to Seton Hall, Miami, and St. John's. I liked the idea of staying in New York City. Reggie Jessie had just committed to St. John's, and I loved their coach, Fran Fraschilla. Playing at St. John's would allow me to stay close to my family, my girlfriend, and my newborn baby daughter, Sadie, so in March I announced that I'd be attending St. John's.

There was one last thing to do before leaving high school and it was probably one of the highlights of my career. I learned that I was invited to play in the McDonald's All-American Game. That meant so much to me. I could have died right there and been okay with my career because I wasn't supposed to make that team. There were a lot of politics involved so it was a long shot. I knew Elton and Lamar would make it because they were two of the best players in the country, but I had to work for my spot.

The game was in Colorado Springs, and from the moment I got there I had an incredible experience. I even entered the dunk contest and had a couple good ones, too. For my first dunk, I jumped from the foul line—well, one foot in from the foul line. I had another dunk where my teammate Anthony Perry threw me an alley-oop from out of bounds. He was from Jersey City and played for Bobby Hurley Sr. at Saint Anthony's. We had a good relationship going into our senior year, so it was pretty cool when he was on my team for the McDonald's game.

The game itself was laid-back. It was basically a scrimmage but the experience was sick. Being able to put on that uniform and go through warmups was the best feeling I'd ever had on the court. It made me realize how far I had come. Even the food and the hotel—it was all great. That experience was one of the highlights of my life. It really felt like I accomplished something, and I couldn't wait to take that feeling with me to St. John's.

Chapter 9

Ron Artest
Goes to College

I was the first person in my family to go to college. I didn't know exactly what I was in for, but I knew I was in for an adjustment.

St. John's didn't have dorms. It was all off-campus living. I found out later that this was a lot different from most of the other schools out there. There was an NCAA rule that allowed any scholarship athlete who lived off campus to receive a room-and-board stipend. We got something like $800 a month to pay for living expenses, so I shared an apartment with Reggie Jessie. That allowed us to split the cost and we could pocket a little bit more of that money. Kimsha and Sadie also came to stay with me, which was cool. They weren't supposed to be there, but they stayed with me anyway. Unfortunately I didn't get to spend much time with them because I was never home. I was either at school or practice.

The only problem with where we lived was that we were so far away from the school and the gym. It was a 30-minute walk, one we had to make when we couldn't get a ride or didn't have money for a cab. That was especially hard in the winter, but we couldn't afford a car. It was one of those little things that make college life difficult, but for the most part college was fun. I had a great time.

Back when I was 14 or 15 I would get drunk on New Year's Eve. I started to drink with my friends at night when I was 16. We'd go play basketball and drink. Now at St. John's I was going out to clubs and doing a bunch of stuff that I wasn't supposed to be doing. We'd use whatever money we had left from our stipend on alcohol. Some nights I was a fucking fool. We weren't going out every night, but when I did I tended to go overboard.

When Sadie wasn't staying with me at the apartment, sometimes we'd throw parties. One time it got completely out of control. Fifty people showed up, including this guy with a shoebox full of marijuana. We smoked the whole damn thing that night. There was smoke everywhere. The neighbors didn't get too upset. I'm surprised, because there was loud music and a lot of marijuana.

There were a couple practices when I showed up smelling like alcohol, but I was still a focused player. I'd eat oatmeal in the morning. I'd eat my beans and rice. I made sure I was healthy. Basketball had always been my number one priority, and it still was when I got to college, but partying quickly became number two. Schoolwork fell to number three. I still wanted to be an architect. I did my best to get in the right classes and put in the work. I remember people on the team telling me not to take certain classes because they were too hard. *Get out of my face. I know it's going to be hard. Sign me up.* They knew I wanted to be an architect and I wouldn't let them persuade me otherwise. I had some harsh conversations about that.

The challenges just made me want to do it more and prove those people wrong. That part I liked, but it was hard for me to take the classes I needed in my major and still go to practice. There were a lot of projects, and during the season I was traveling with the team, so I fell behind. Eventually I had to switch out of some of those classes or I would have failed off the team. That's why I changed my major to math.

On the court, the St. John's basketball team was coming off a losing season, but expectations were high for us to do much better. My expectations for the team were even higher. I had just played for a team that went 27–0 and won a city championship, so that's where my head was at. I wanted to go to the Final Four and win a national championship.

More than anything else, I was excited to play for Fran Fraschilla. Fran was very passionate and he was very smart— probably one of the smartest people I'd ever been around. He was like a professor of basketball and he knew exactly what it took to make us the best we could be. He pushed us in a way that Kobe Bryant pushed the players on his Lakers teams. And like with Kobe, playing for Fran was very much a sink-or-swim situation. If you couldn't keep up with him, you wouldn't make it. That pressure was too much for some people. You had to have a thick skin.

Fran was from Brooklyn so he wouldn't back down from anyone. He was only 5'7", but he would yell and scream at us like he was the biggest guy on the court. He made sure to let us know who was in charge. He always said, "When you coach a New York City player, the coach has to be crazier than he is." The funny thing is that Fran would yell and get in our faces, but we could go right back at him and he would be able to take it. Most coaches can't do that. One time I got right up in his face and was ready to fight. He wouldn't sit us just because we yelled back or stood up to him. He didn't hold a grudge, but he didn't let us off the hook either. When we did stupid shit he disciplined us. Fran was crazy, but I was crazy too, so we got along great and had some good times that year. I love Fran.

Training camp was insane. The conditioning he made us do was unreal. There was this one drill called 20-20. It started with everyone running a suicide. The point guards had to finish in 28 seconds, shooting guards in 30, forwards in 32, and centers in 34. When you finished you'd get a 30-second rest and then have to run another. We had to run 20 suicides total. If you didn't finish one in time, that was one more that you'd have to run at the end. If you weren't careful, you'd be there all day running suicides. And if you didn't finish that day, you'd have to show up early in the morning the next day before practice to get them all done. That's what almost happened to me the first couple of times I did that drill. I wasn't finishing in time so our strength and conditioning coach, Coach Al, got right up in my face and challenged me. He made me do it again and held up the entire team until I finished in time. I got so mad at him, but he earned my respect by pushing me.

There were days when I thought I was literally going to die because the coaches pushed us so hard. We all wanted to quit, but Fran wouldn't let us. We didn't have a choice. Those practices before the start of the season took their toll mentally and physically. I don't think I've ever been pushed to the limit the way Fran pushed me. That's a hell of a compliment because I consider myself a relentlessly hard worker. But he got more out of me than any other coach. When it came to being the best and getting ready to play in the NBA, I credit Fran with providing me with that blueprint.

My freshman year was the first time I had set foot in a weight room. I had always been naturally strong, and lifting weights made me a lot bigger. I think I was about 225 pounds when I first arrived at St. John's. Under Fran, I was able to get up to 250. We were also running hard every day, so I didn't lose any quickness and I wasn't getting fat. I was putting on crazy muscle.

Going to St. John's also allowed me to play alongside New York City basketball royalty in Felipe Lopez. He was older than me, so I never played with him or against him back in high school. But I used to watch him when I could and I was always in awe. Once I saw him jump from the free throw line and dunk in a game. Now he was a senior and the leader of our team, but I had no idea why he was even in college. He should have been in the NBA. The college game was not for him but he stayed all four years. *What the hell?* That was insane to me. He was very competitive so I'm sure he wanted to win an NCAA title, but he was the top player coming out of high school. He was bigger than LeBron James at the time, and this was way before social media and Twitter. Going to college hurt him. Teams would triple-team him and make him look bad. He always had NBA ability and he still made it to the league, but I don't know why he spent so much time in college.

We had the opportunity to practice with some former St. John's players who had gone on to the NBA. Chris Mullin and Mark Jackson would come to the gym and play with us, as would Malik Sealey and Shawnelle Scott. They may have been pros but we had a really good team. We were different from most college teams and were crazy, so those games weren't easy for them. We made sure that they got some good work in.

The summer before my freshman year, Jayson Williams came down to play pickup games with us. Jayson was 6'10" and about 270 pounds, and he used to tell us that he was the strongest player in the league. He might have been. He was big and he had an even bigger personality. Jayson was great. Off the court, he treated us like little brothers, but he treated us like men when we stepped onto the court. He tried to push us and would call us out if he didn't think we were putting in effort.

"I drove two hours to get here," he once told us. "If you aren't gonna play hard I can get back in my car and drive home. If you wanna make the NBA, it starts right now. I can show you, but that will never happen if you don't play hard."

That rubbed me the wrong way. I didn't like anybody questioning my effort or toughness. So when he got the ball on a breakaway, I ran as hard as I could and chased him down. Nobody was getting an easy dunk, especially after what he just said. I wanted to foul him hard, but we jumped at the same time so I ended up clotheslining him. It wasn't meant to be a dirty play, just a hard foul. He hit the ground. I looked down at him and said, "Is that hard enough?"

I think that might have surprised some of the guys on my team. It even surprised Jayson a little bit, but we were cool. We finished the game and everything was fine. Those games were physical, and the pros like Jayson really helped make our team tough.

When the regular season began I wasn't in the starting lineup. I came off the bench, but I knew that I would start if I continued to play hard. I played well in our first two games against Lafayette and St. Francis, but those were smaller schools that we were expected to beat. We then flew down to Puerto Rico for a tournament before the start of the Big East schedule. Before we left, Fran said he was going to put me in the starting lineup. He wanted to do it when we were on the road so I wouldn't have the pressure of starting my first game in front of a home crowd at Madison Square Garden.

We stayed at a resort and tried to relax and have fun, but I was still there to win. I wanted to prove to everyone that I belonged on the team and I deserved to be a starter. During that first game against American University of Puerto Rico, I came out and dropped 24 points and grabbed six rebounds. I tried to get everyone involved and distribute the ball to our scorers. I also had a couple of big dunks, too. There were probably fewer than a hundred people in that gym, but it was hot. It felt like it was over 100 degrees in there, so it was tough for me to catch my breath. Even Fran's shirt was soaked with sweat by the end of that game.

We lost the next game to Georgia Tech, who ended up winning the tournament. They had Matt Harpring, who went on to be a pretty good pro. This was our first test against a big school and it showed us that we had a lot of work to do. But at least I proved that I could play.

Making the transition from high school to college wasn't as difficult for me personally as the previous transition into high school was. I didn't have to adjust my game at all. The players were better and the game moved faster, but I was a hard worker so it wasn't difficult. The upperclassmen took me under their wing and helped me out a lot. I wanted to be an important part of that team, but I didn't speak out of turn and always deferred to the seniors when it came to leading the team. I used to ask them a ton of questions about everything. Guys like Tarik Turner looked out for me, and I would often room with Tarik when we were on the road. I still keep in touch with him to this day. I have to thank those guys for making the transition easier for me.

That said, I struggled at times. The problems I experienced in college were the same ones I had experienced in high school. I still couldn't score like some of the other top players in the country. I saw some other freshmen, like Larry Hughes at Saint Louis University, scoring 40 points in one game. *Damn, he can score.* Me, I was getting like 11 points.

During that season, Fran would try to get under my skin. It worked, too. He'd always drop f-bombs and call us soft. He'd tell us we were playing scared and that we didn't want to win badly enough. And Fran didn't care who was listening. Father James Maher was the campus minister. He traveled with the team so he was always in the locker room. Fran would scream at us and say all these things that he probably shouldn't have said in front of Father Maher. Poor Father Maher was just sitting there. He was a great guy. I love Father Maher, but sometimes he didn't know what to do when Fran went off.

Fran had a rule that freshmen couldn't speak to the media until after their first semester, so that kept me from saying anything stupid. There were no fights or blowups during practice either. It almost felt like Fran would beat us to the punch. Whenever things got rough in practice, he would be the one to blow up. "Get the hell out of my practice!" he'd yell. And he meant it, too. We had to walk out of the gym and he'd be screaming at us the whole way. One time, he kicked the door so hard that it hit me on the way out.

Fran held us all accountable. Nobody got star treatment. In early January we had just come off a loss to Seton Hall and were 9–5. We spent the next couple practices getting ready for our game against Louisville. I don't even remember exactly what happened. I don't think it was anything out of the ordinary, but I showed up to practice a couple minutes late. Fran didn't care. He said I couldn't start against Louisville.

We finished 22–10 that year, second in the Big East. We made it to the NCAA tournament as a seven seed but got upset by Detroit Mercy in a close first-round game that came down to the wire. That was disappointing, especially for the seniors. I think we might have overlooked Detroit Mercy and had our sights set on a matchup with No. 2 Purdue. It was difficult to lose, but that was the furthest St. John's had made it in a while, so we definitely felt like we had a good year and were going in the right direction. I wish we could have gone deeper into the tournament for those seniors, but those guys helped us turn the program around. My whole NCAA tournament experience that year was a blur. It came and went so quickly. Before I knew it, we were out of it and our season was over.

The most disappointing part of the season was when Fran was fired in May of 1998. That made me upset because Fran was a big reason that I went to St. John's. It all happened pretty fast. After the season, we knew something was going on when Fran didn't show up at the awards banquet. We then had a team meeting with the athletics director and he told us what happened. It's not that Fran wasn't a good coach. He turned the program around, recruited great players, and won 22 games that year. Coaches who do that usually don't get fired, but I don't think people could handle Fran because he was so intense. I personally thought they should have kept him. Fran went on to coach for the University of New Mexico, which is where Eric Chatfield wound up transferring after attending junior college. It was crazy that both Eric and I played for Fran during our college careers, but at two different schools. Fran now works for ESPN covering college basketball, but I really want to see him get back into coaching.

In the summer, I went right back home and played street-ball again. I always wanted to get better, but that summer I tried a little too hard. I overworked my jump shot, doing too much shooting instead of working on a bunch of different things. Looking back, what I really needed was more rest. I didn't learn that until later in my career. I'd see guys sit out some practices and actually end up doing better in the game. Finally, it dawned on me. *Oh, it's because they have their legs.* I was always tired during the games, but I managed to push through it. Even later, when I was in the NBA, there were a lot of times when I was tired because I was trying to do too much.

In June, St. John's hired Mike Jarvis as the new head coach. Just like Fran, Jarvis had a lot of success coaching at a smaller school. He had just come from George Washington, where he had taken his team to the Sweet Sixteen. He was an NBA-ready coach, but he was much different from Fran. I learned a lot from both of my coaches in college, but I personally did better with Fran because of the way he pushed me. I tried to remember that and keep the same intensity, especially during practice, but not having Fran hurt me a little as a player. With Fran, it was always about basketball. He was detail-orientated and insisted we do every single thing right. He pushed us until we were exhausted, but everybody got better.

With Jarvis, we were more of a relaxed team. He didn't yell and he never lost his cool. It was an atmosphere very similar to the one Phil Jackson created when I was with the Lakers. It was a different concept. Jarvis also brought more of a family atmosphere to the team. We'd go to his house, where his wife would cook for us. She'd always be around. When

I got sick, she made this big pot of chicken noodle soup for me. She was definitely like a mom to everyone.

My sophomore year we had a smaller and younger team, but we were tough. I'm not going to say that we were better because we had lost Felipe to the NBA, but we did add Bootsy Thornton to the lineup. He was a 6'4" shooting guard originally from West Baltimore. Bootsy was a junior and had actually been on the team the previous year, but he had to sit out because he had transferred from community college. After that loss to Detroit Mercy in the NCAA tournament the previous year, I pulled him aside and told him, "We'll be back here next year and you're going to be a big part of this team. We need you."

We also had Erick Barkley that year. Erick went to prep school at Maine Central Institute right out of high school to improve his grades, so he was coming into St. John's as a freshman. He had just made the McDonald's All-American team and he really was a coach's dream. I can honestly say that Erick was probably one of the best point guards I've ever played with. He was amazing on defense. He could shoot and was quick to the basket.

I wanted to make it to the Final Four and I wanted to win the national championship. I knew we could do it because we had a team that was talented enough. We just had to find a way to put it all together. In the back of my mind I knew there was a chance that this would be my last season and that I'd be leaving for the NBA. If we were going to go all the way, it had to be this year. I wanted to go out on top, so I tried to keep doing all the same things that had gotten me to that point. My role as a player never changed. The coaches for every team I was on stressed defense and playing like a team, which was how I played. I felt that I could take over games when I had to, but I always played the game the same way.

93

That season we got off to a quick 3–0 start with a big win over a ranked UMass team, but then during the preseason NIT we lost two games in a row to Stanford and Purdue. Both teams were highly ranked, but we could have won those games. They were both really close. I was mad and I let the rest of the team hear about it. I may have been young, but I considered myself the leader of that team. To me, that meant calling people out. By then, I didn't care if someone was an upperclassman or older than me. I didn't care if I had to be the bad guy.

We were playing well and we had a good record, but I just couldn't get used to losing. I had only lost a handful of games my entire career until college. Losing reveals your character—for better or worse. It did get me back into the gym and working harder to get better, but it mostly brought out the absolute worst in me. I'd break things in the locker rooms. I'd disrupt practice by getting into arguments and fights. At the time I thought I was being a leader, but looking back at it now I was being selfish. I yelled. I lashed out. I got physical. Whenever I felt that somebody on the team wasn't trying hard or didn't believe in what we were trying to do, I'd get in his face. There were times when it was more about me than the team. I'd blame everyone else and be in the locker room saying things like, "I'm the only one who wants to play in the NBA. You don't and when you play like that you're messing with my money. Work harder!" Fran once told me that I couldn't expect people to work as hard as me. Not everybody is as crazy about basketball or has the same passion. It took me a long time to realize that.

Whatever problems we were having as a team, we worked them out by the end of the season and had a good run in the Big East Tournament. We beat No. 9 Miami and made it to the final but we lost to Connecticut, which was the

No. 3 team in the country. We felt good going into the NCAA tournament. We got a No. 3 seed and played our first two games down in Orlando. We beat Samford and Indiana convincingly. Then we went to Knoxville for the Sweet Sixteen and drew Maryland, which was the No. 2 seed. They had Steve Francis. We weren't supposed to win that game, but we beat them by 14 and advanced to the Elite Eight against Ohio State.

We were one win away from the Final Four and we were playing the best we had all year. It happened so fast. Everybody on the team started to get that feeling. The idea of a national title was a very real possibility at that point.

But as soon as the game started against Ohio State, everything went wrong. I was anxious and picked up an offensive foul right away. I think everyone was anxious because it took both teams forever to score. Ohio State got going first. They had Scoonie Penn, a great college guard. He put them up early with a three-point play and then a four-point play.

I couldn't get it together and I kept losing the ball. In the first 10 minutes I had four turnovers and two fouls. It was frustrating and I guess it showed, because I came out of the game. As a team we weren't playing our typical game and we definitely weren't playing like we had in the first three games of the tournament.

Bootsy Thornton was the only one who played well for us. He had been our leading scorer all year and he was keeping us in the game, but we didn't have an answer for Scoonie Penn or Michael Redd. They were tough, and the second half was more of the same. I kept missing shots. I was getting frustrated. Ohio State was just playing better and pulled ahead.

Ken Johnson scored a couple of buckets over me in the paint. He kept making these little jump hooks that I couldn't do much about because he was 6'11". I took that personally and it might have sparked something inside me because I stepped it up. I wasn't going to let what might be my only shot at a Final Four slip away. I got a quick steal that I passed ahead to Lavor Postell for two. We got another stop, and the next trip down the court Lavor hit a three to put us right back in the game.

We were chipping away. I scored underneath with a minute to play to cut the lead to four. Ohio State was a poor free throw shooting team. I don't know if it's true, but I heard their coach Jim O'Brien hired a sports psychologist to help them at the foul line. We knew that if we kept fouling them we had a chance. It worked. They missed the front end of a couple one-and-ones and we had the ball down two with 12 seconds left. Unfortunately, Scoonie Penn stripped Erick Barkley and that was the game.

Some people blame Erick for that loss and he was so hard on himself after, but it wasn't his fault. That was his only turnover of the game. He helped get us there and set the school record for freshman scoring in that game. I didn't play well. The team didn't play well. It didn't help that me, Erick, and Reggie Jessie all went out to Church's Chicken the night before to eat a bunch of food. That killed our energy and left us sluggish all game. It felt like the state tournament back in high school all over again, but the blame fell on us. It was a disappointing loss but we had a great run. St. John's has not gotten that far in the tournament since.

That season I was named first-team All–Big East and third-team All-American. I knew I had a chance to be really good. I knew I could be better than a lot of the All-Stars in the NBA. I had the work ethic. I just didn't know how long it would take me to get there.

After the season, I had to decide if I was going to stay in school. I talked with Mike Jarvis, but I also spoke with Bill

Aberer, Mr. Lorch, my parents, and Hank Carter, because they were all a big reason why I had gotten that far. A lot of them wanted to see me finish school, but the chance to make money playing in the NBA was difficult to pass up. Finally I sat down with Kimsha and we decided that it was time for me to leave St. John's. College was definitely fun but I needed to move on. I already had one child and Kimsha was pregnant again, so my decision to leave was also financial. I had an obligation and a family to support. Jarvis did some research for me. He told me where I was projected to go and there was a good chance I'd be a lottery pick. He gave me a lot of advice along the way.

I have always been the type of person to go overboard, so when it came time to announce my decision, I wanted to do it in style and make a big public announcement. I could have kept it more low-key but that's not who I am. I held a press conference at the community center to announce my decision to enter the NBA draft. After that press conference my mom threw a big party back at the apartment. It was great to see everyone from the block there. All my family and friends were there, but what really touched me was seeing how proud my brothers and sisters were of me. Something about announcing that decision made the idea of being a pro basketball player seem a little more real for them. They really believed in me, and I think that also helped them realize they too could do anything they put their minds to.

I may have thought I was ready for the NBA because I was successful on the court, but I was only 19. I was still very young and immature. Mentally, I was an emotional wreck. I was making a ton of mistakes and my life felt like it was in shambles. I couldn't really let things go. Every little thing bothered me. That season, Mike Jarvis and Father Maher introduced me to a counselor named Dr. Raymond DeGuesspe to help me deal with my anger. He tried to make me realize that I couldn't control everything. The one thing I could control for the time being was basketball, so that's where I tried to channel my aggression.

I had this idea throughout college that turning pro and getting that financial security would solve a lot of my problems. I didn't realize it at the time, but there were so many more lessons I had left to learn.

Making it to the NBA was only the beginning.

CHICAGO

Chapter 10

The Rookie

At one point I was projected to be a top-10 pick in the 1999 NBA Draft.

It was a big night for me so I arranged for two busloads of people from the hood to be picked up and brought to the hotel we were staying at in Washington, D.C. There were like 50 of us there, which is kind of crazy, but I wanted to have fun. I've always felt that it's important to remember where I came from. I put a lot of pressure on myself to stay true to my roots and not change who I was just because I had found some success.

The draft was held at the MCI Center, which is now called the Verizon Center. All the players projected to go early were there, including Elton Brand and Lamar Odom. The three of us started playing together as kids, and there we were sitting in the same room at the NBA draft. That was pretty unbelievable.

I sat at a table with my mom and Kimsha. It was exciting but it was also nerve-racking, because there was nothing I could do—I just had to sit there and wait for my name to be called. It felt like we were sitting around forever before the draft actually started. Finally, NBA commissioner David Stern stepped to the podium to announce the first pick. The Bulls drafted Elton, which I thought was cool because the Bulls were my favorite team growing up.

Nobody realized at the time how good the players in this draft would turn out to be. Many went on to have great careers and left their mark on the league. I'm proud to be a part of that, but at the time I was anxious to see where I was going. I knew it would be a little while before my name was called, but I had done the math in my head. I figured that I would go 13th, at the latest. The Knicks had the 15th pick and I would love to have been selected by the Knicks, but I didn't think I'd drop that far.

The Vancouver Grizzlies took Steve Francis second and Baron Davis went third to the Charlotte Hornets. Both were amazing players. Fourth was Lamar, who went to the Los Angeles Clippers. Jonathan Bender, who came right out of high school, went to the Toronto Raptors. He might have had a really good NBA career but he injured his knee. Wally Sczcerbiak and Richard Hamilton went sixth and seventh. Andre Miller was next, and he went on to be one of the all-time assist leaders. Shawn Marion and Jason Terry followed, and they both played for a very long time. Trajon Langdon from Duke went 11th. He was a great college player, but he had a short pro career.

Suddenly we were up to the 12th pick and I was getting nervous because my name could be called at any time. My mom and Kimsha tried to keep me calm, but it's hard not to get caught up in the whole experience no matter how much you try to stay grounded.

The Raptors selected Aleksandar Radojević from Yugoslavia at No. 12, who I hadn't even heard of before. Two Duke Blue Devils, Corey Maggette and William Avery, went 13th and 14th. At that point I was like, *Okay, what's going on here.* I was slipping.

When you're sitting there at the draft waiting for your name to be called, that is exactly what you don't want to happen. But there was an upside. The Knicks were on the clock with the 15th pick. Obviously, I wanted to go to the Knicks. New York was in my blood and playing at home was starting to look like a very real possibility. That was exciting.

When David Stern returned to the podium, he announced that the Knicks had selected Frédéric Weis.

Who?

Weis was a 7'2" big man from France who later became known as the guy Vince Carter dunked over in the 2000 Olympics. He never came over to play in the NBA. Before I even had a chance to get upset or feel disappointed, I heard David Stern call my name: I was selected with the 16th pick by the Chicago Bulls. I found out right then and there when my name was announced. There were no phone calls or warning signals beforehand. I was now a Bull.

That was something that I never expected. It meant that I would be playing with Elton on my favorite pro team. I couldn't believe my luck. Two friends who played together in high school get picked by the same team in the same draft? It was like a dream come true.

I walked on stage and shook David Stern's hand for the first time. I was crying. I don't know why. It just felt cool to be drafted at the time. Bulls GM Jerry Krause would later say that he really liked the way I was willing to sacrifice my own offensive game for the good of the team. Yeah, I think I should have been taken sooner, but it's hard for general managers to know who is going to be good, so they have to guess. It's not important where you get taken in the draft. What's important is what you do when you get to the league. People forget that Andrei Kirilenko and Manu Ginobili were also in that draft, so you never know. For me, everything worked out in the end.

That night we went back to the hotel and had a good time. I tried to enjoy myself and chill with my family. Soon after, I signed a three-year deal that would pay me around $3 million.

The first thing I did was go back to the hood and hook up my mom's crib. I wanted to buy her a new house, but my mom never wanted to leave the hood. So I put about $60,000 into fixing up her place. We had little steps into a red room and TVs all over the place.

Once my mom was squared away, I moved to Libertyville, a suburb about 30 minutes outside of Chicago. I was always skeptical of being next to the projects, so I stayed as far away as possible, but Libertyville was so far that I later had to move closer to the city. I got an apartment in Highland Park and soon after that I bought a house in Chicago for like $300,000. That was by far my biggest purchase.

I didn't set out to spend a lot of money. I was happy to have the chance to help a lot of my people out, but I wanted to keep things modest. I did need a car, though. At first I wanted to buy a Caravan, but somebody on my team was like, "You can't be driving around in no Caravan." He told me to buy a Suburban instead. So that's what I did and it was all downhill from there.

Right after the draft my agent arranged for me to go down to Miami to work out and get ready for my rookie season. It was great to be in a place where I could get away and just play. I also got the chance to work out with Randy Moss and Cris Carter from the Minnesota Vikings. We'd do some weight training together and run sprints. That was amazing. Randy Moss was only a couple years older than me and had been in the NFL for just two years, but he was already an absolute beast.

For one of the drills, we tried to reach top speed while running on the incline treadmill. Randy got up to 21 miles per hour. I could only get up to 14. I knew Randy was fast, but I had no idea he was that fast. That was insane. It's completely different when you see it up close.

I learned what work ethic was really all about by watching Cris Carter. He was older at the time, but he was still working so hard on every single drill. He didn't let up at all. I always considered myself a hard worker, and I was, but watching those two made me realize that you had to keep pushing yourself and that you could always go harder.

I got to play some ball with them, too. Randy was actually a good basketball player. He could really jump—he was out there dunking like it was nothing. Back when he was in high school, he played with Jason Williams in West Virginia. Randy could have been really good if he kept at it, but his future was in football.

I had returned to New York when I learned that my son Ron was born. Kimsha and I were still together but we were going through some issues. Being a parent was tough for me at first because I didn't fully understand what that involved. I was immature because I was still a kid myself. I matured as I got older, but it was difficult for me to put in the time and be there when I needed to be. As parents, we weren't in the ideal situation. Looking back on things, I wasn't ready for the responsibility but we made it work.

Pretty soon it was time for training camp. I couldn't believe how much had changed so quickly. A few months earlier I was in college. Now I was a professional basketball player making a lot of money on the Chicago Bulls. I'd just had my second child. Things were moving fast.

Tim Floyd was our head coach. He had coached at Iowa State and then was hired by the Bulls in 1998 to replace Phil Jackson after Chicago's dynasty ended. I was excited to get started, but that first training camp was tough. Floyd approached practice the way a college coach would—he worked us hard and there was a lot of screaming. That was fine by me; after all, I had played for Fran. I went in just wanting to be the absolute best I could be.

I knew that I could be great, but I didn't have a clear-cut plan on how to do that. The one thing that I did know how to do was put in the effort. My effort was the one thing I could control, so I went hard. When we did drills, I ran as fast as I could. Even when I got tired, I pushed through. Still, I couldn't do everything that I wanted to offensively. I had some bad shooting days. It took me a while to learn how to shoot and develop an offensive game that could translate to the NBA. I had some decent moves, but in the NBA you have to be efficient and smart. The problem was that I never developed strong fundamentals. I had a high basketball IQ and that helped mask some of my offensive weaknesses, but the lack of fundamentals really held me back. I needed those skills in order to be the type of player that I knew I could be.

The biggest change for me was the speed of the game. In the NBA, you have to make decisions fast. For a while I didn't know what the hell I was doing. It's always frustrating when you aren't able to go out there and do what you want to do. I now realize that was a source of many of my problems and one of the reasons why I lashed out so often during those first few years in Chicago.

The guys in the NBA were older and way more advanced than I was, but defensively I was solid. I was one of the better defenders in the league at an early age. No matter what was happening on the offensive side of the ball, I felt that I was really good at disrupting the other team on the defensive end. My defense was ready from day one, but it was Tim Floyd who helped take that to the next level. I have him to thank for how I developed as a defensive player in the NBA, because as good as I was as a defender, it was the lack of those fundamentals that prevented me from being the absolute best. He's the one who taught me how to really lock people up at the NBA level. He helped with my footwork and conditioning. Those were things that I hadn't even thought about on my own, but improving those areas took me to another level. We didn't always see eye to eye, but he was probably the best coach I ever had when it came to teaching individual defense.

It took me a long time to get over the fact that I was actually playing for the Chicago Bulls. They were my favorite team growing up. The first time I met B.J. Armstrong, I told him about seeing him hit that shot on TV when I was younger. B.J. played well for us that year, even though he missed some time because he had bad knees. He and Toni Kukoc were our vets. Toni was also hurt. He had a bad back and it took him a while to recover, but he kept us working hard.

One thing that was very different about this new Bulls team compared to the ones I remember watching on TV was that we were not winning. Phil Jackson was gone. So were Jordan and Pippen. We were back at square one. We weren't expected to win many games and that was hard for me to stomach. It's hard to prepare yourself for dealing with so many losses. I thought losing at St. John's was difficult, but we finished 28–9 during my final season in college. My rookie year with the Bulls, we were 17–65. I hadn't lost that many games in my entire career up to that point. We were the worst team in the league. Dead last.

That whole year I just did not feel good about myself. Losing put me in survival mode where I was just like, *Fuck it.* And it's not like it came and went quickly; the NBA season is a long grind. The regular season starts in October and ends in April. It's even longer when you're eating poorly and partying too much. Taking care of your body is something else you learn when you get older, but when you're young, sometimes you have to learn these lessons the hard way. The veterans can show you the ropes, but to really understand and appreciate what they're talking about you have to live through it.

I also had to get used to the weather. New York was cold, but Chicago was colder. You could feel that cold inside the arena when you were playing. I got in the habit of changing my game jersey at halftime. Most players only wear one jersey per game, but I hated being sweaty and cold, so I'd do a full uniform change for the second half. Everything except for my shoes. That uniform change became a habit that I kept for most of my career.

Personally, I had a decent year. I was able to average 12 points per game, but a lot of those were garbage points. I was named to the All-Rookie second team, but that recognition didn't mean much. There were some great rookies who didn't get to play that much because they were on good teams. I don't think Ginobili made any of those rookie teams, and look at the career he went on to have. I like to think that if I had been on a winning team when I entered the league that I would have played better and felt better about myself, but there is no guarantee that I'd be getting enough playing time on a better team. If I had to sit, that would get me upset, too.

No rookie in the league had a better year than Elton. He was so good that he had no trouble transitioning into the league. He was definitely ready. The NBA was a perfect fit for him. He was our leading scorer. He averaged 20 points and 10 rebounds and was named Rookie of the Year. Against the Utah Jazz at the United Center, he converted on 14 straight field goals for us, something that beat one of Jordan's records. When I saw him do that I realized that I was watching a superstar develop. *How did he get so good?*

That's why I was confused when the Bulls traded him in 2001 to the Clippers for Brian Skinner and the draft rights to Tyson Chandler. *What are they thinking?* Elton wasn't unhappy. He didn't demand a trade. He wasn't trouble—he was the opposite. He was also probably one of the most mature players I ever played with. Maybe they were trying to get more athletic. I don't know. If it were up to me I would have kept him, but it wasn't up to me.

During the season I stayed in Chicago, but in the summertime I would return to Queens. I had rented a little condo off the LIE. Now that I was a pro and was making money, I wanted to give back to my community. In the summer of 2001 I returned to the Five-Star Basketball Camp in Pennsylvania. I got to see some old coaches and counselors while I hung around for a couple days to work the camp and help the kids.

By this time, Kimsha and I had separated. She had been living with me in Chicago but moved back to New York with Sadie and Ron. I had started seeing Jennifer, who I met back at St. John's. Jennifer was pregnant and I got the call when I was down at Five-Star that she had given birth to our son, Jeron. I left the camp and went to New York City to meet my new son. Later that year, Jenny and Jeron came out to live with me in Chicago.

In the off-season, a bunch of us used to play in Chicago at Hoops the Gym. I always liked to play ball, and I didn't care where or when. I knew a bunch of pros used to go over there so when I got the opportunity to play with them, of course I went. Michael Finley, Jerry Stackhouse, Ray Allen, Tim Hardaway, Juwan Howard, and Antoine Walker would be there. Charles Barkley showed up a couple times. A 15-year-old LeBron James would play with us, and he was killing it. Even as a teenager playing against pros, he could hold his own.

But the guy who organized those games and was there every day was Michael Jordan. He had just announced his return from his second retirement and would be playing for the Washington Wizards the following season, but during the summer he was out in Chicago and working hard. Jordan was really something else. He had always been super competitive, but from what I saw of him that summer I thought he might even get MVP the following year.

Whenever I matched up against him, I tried to never let him breathe. I made sure to be all over him. He liked that and he always wanted me to come to the gym. We were talking after a pickup game once and he told me, "I wish I could have played against you when I was younger." I took that as a big compliment. Of course, he'd still score because he was so damn good. Jordan played hard all the time and those games were some of the toughest games I played in. Those games made me so much better.

That's why I was so upset when I learned that I had broken Michael's ribs.

I always played hard but I never meant to injure him. I saw one report that claimed I bodyslammed him to the ground, but it didn't happen like that. Not at all. It happened during a pickup game in the summer of 2001. Jordan was posting me up on the right block. He was so strong that it was hard to get in front of him. It seemed like he scored every time he got the ball, so the best way to stop him was to prevent him from getting the ball in the first place. That's what I was trying to do, but he had his left arm holding me back. We were battling. I used my right arm to try and get his left arm out of the way, but my elbow hit him in the ribs. I could tell something happened because of the way he grunted. He was holding his ribs on his way down the court. It looked like he was going to take himself out of the game, but he stayed in and then drained a 15-foot jumper off the dribble to win the game. Then he walked off the court.

I went home that day and thought everything was cool. Then I got a call and learned that I had broken Michael Jordan's ribs. I didn't leave the house for two days. I couldn't believe it. Jordan had just come out of retirement and was playing so well, and now I was going to get blamed for possibly ending his career for good. All kinds of thoughts went through my head.

On that third day, Jordan called me himself. I wasn't expecting that at all. I didn't recognize the number when I answered the phone.

"Can I speak to Ron?" came the voice on the other side.

"Who's this?"

"It's M.J."

"I'm so sorry about what happened."

"Don't worry about it."

"My bad, I was just playing hard."

"I know. Things happen. Forget about it."

And that was it. Hearing from Jordan made me feel a little better about the whole thing. I finally left my house and went to the gym that day to work out.

The rib injury knocked Jordan out for three months. When he came back, he went on to average 22.9 points per game that season. To average 22.9 points coming off broken ribs at his age was unbelievable. What could he have done if he was healthy the whole year? I felt like such an asshole, because if he didn't get hurt he might have averaged 30 or 35.

Chapter 11

Hennessy Has No Place in the Locker Room

When I got to the NBA people told me that I had made it, but the only way I had made it was financially. I hadn't won anything. In fact, I was pretty far behind in the game of life. I was not ready for the league or for the lifestyle that came with it.

I went from making nothing to making a million dollars a year. I had a great support system but I wasn't listening to them all the time. I think I lost some of those family values when I got to the league because there was so much going on. Fame gets to you a little bit. I was getting recognized when I played at St. John's, but being an NBA player was completely different. The real problem was having the money that allowed me the freedom to do almost anything I wanted.

Now, it wasn't all bad, because the money did allow me to help a lot of the people close to me, but there was also a lot of partying going on. It's easy to get wrapped up in that and lose yourself. That's what happened to me in Chicago. All of a sudden, I could buy all the Cristal I wanted. I'd be buying out bars and doing a bunch of crazy shit. Weed all over the damn place. I was tripping out. My man Cedric from 12th Street was staying with me, and I told him that his only job was to make sure there was a big bowl filled with blunts when I got home.

I got bigheaded. I let that money change me, rather than staying the same person I had always been. That's not the ideal situation when you have children who you need to be there for. I wasn't ready to be a professional. I wasn't a gangster like some people may have thought, but I was always into the street life, so behaving like a professional didn't interest me much.

There are a lot of stories out there about my time in Chicago. Some of them are true. Not all of them, though. I heard one story about me stripping down naked at halftime to yell at some of my Bulls teammates. I don't remember that one happening so don't believe everything you hear.

The one that a lot of people ask me about is whether I really applied for a job at Circuit City. That one is absolutely true. I applied for the job mainly because I was bored. Here I was, fresh out of college and living in Chicago. This was at a time when my kids were living in New York. I had a couple friends coming out to live with me, but there wasn't much for me to do outside of practice. I was used to being surrounded by people with tons of things going on. There was none of that out there in the suburbs. I didn't know what to do with myself. Cedric had a job at Circuit City, so I thought I would apply there, too. Plus, employees got a nice discount. I walked right into the store and asked the manager if I could fill out an application. I put the Bulls down as a reference. Then it got out in the media and people made it seem like I was crazy.

I wasn't doing anything wrong, but I quickly realized that I probably shouldn't be doing stuff like that. Maybe it was a little crazy, but I was young and not thinking that far ahead.

I also wasn't thinking that clearly and was going through some difficult times. I experienced what must have been some kind of mental breakdown when I was in Chicago. It happened when I was driving on the highway. Something came over me and I had to pull over and I just started crying. Nothing specific had happened to trigger that feeling, but at that moment everything that was going on just got to be too much. I was losing control. I had all this baby mama drama. I always knew that I wanted to be a good partner and a good father, but I just wasn't acting like one and it bothered me a lot. I felt like I was losing my family. Instead of being positive and working to improve my situation, I became self-destructive.

That was around the time when I drank Hennessy in the locker room. Yes, this was something that actually happened, but it only happened once. It wasn't something I did all the time. I was in the locker room before a game, and instead of going out onto the court to shootaround after putting on my warmups, I walked straight out of the stadium to the liquor store down the street. The bell over the door chimed when I walked inside. I looked at the old man behind the counter and said, "Give me some Hennessy right now." He looked at me crooked. He knew who I was. Hell, I had my name on the back of my shirt. It took him a little while to ring up the transaction, but he did. On my walk back to the stadium, some of the alcoholics on the street were waving to me and calling out my name. I walked right back into the locker room and started drinking.

It was self-destructive and completely irresponsible, but that's how I chose to deal with my own frustrations. I wasn't making good decisions. The Bulls never found out about that particular incident, but they knew I was struggling. They tried offering me many different forms of help. They even got me a psychiatrist who prescribed me this medicine that was supposed to help me calm down. I was skeptical of any kind of medication, because I saw how my dad had been affected by the pills he'd been prescribed. That's why I immediately asked the psychiatrist, "Are these going to change the way I play at all?" He assured me that they wouldn't.

I took those pills one time but I didn't like how they made me feel. They actually made me feel worse and it took me a while to get back to feeling like my old self. It was bad. I flushed the rest of the pills down the toilet and made the decision to figure my shit out on my own.

Pills might not have been the answer, but I still hadn't learned how to embrace the support I was being offered. I felt that I was invincible and strong enough to do it all on my own. Physically I was strong, but nobody is strong enough to overpower their own emotions. Unfortunately, my stubbornness led to me drinking more alcohol and smoking more weed. That didn't make anything better. I realize now that drinking and smoking held me back those first few years in the league. I had decent numbers, but those numbers would have been much better and I would have been more productive had I taken better care of myself.

My third year with the Bulls was more of the same. The 2001 season got off to a bad start. By the end of December we were 4–21. Tim Floyd stepped down on Christmas Eve and assistant coach Bill Cartwright took his place. It was great to play for a legend like that. He had five rings and he had been an assistant with the Bulls dating back to the Phil Jackson era. I guess there had been talk of Bill replacing Phil a few years earlier, rather than Tim Floyd, but he had to undergo a couple of operations to repair his voice.

As a team we started to play better, but we were still losing a lot. I was settling down and having a much better year but my attitude was still lousy. I racked up a lot of hard flagrant fouls. I'd do things like give fans the middle finger when they would yell stuff. I even gave the finger to the crowd in Chicago a few times. That was a bit excessive. The real problem I had was getting into it with other players when it was unnecessary. I did that a lot and that's what I'm most upset about. Back home, that's how we played basketball. We'd always get into it with each other. I carried that style of play with me to the NBA. I can recognize the problems that it caused now, but when I was going through it I didn't take the time to analyze where the problem was coming from.

Tensions on the team were high, but Bill Cartwright looked out for me. During one road trip, he came into my hotel room and had a heart-to-heart. Something had gotten on my nerves a few games earlier, I don't recall exactly what it was. But I was mad about something and acting out. That happened a lot. It's hard to keep track of everything that happened, and that was part of the problem. It was the same old thing over and over again. The Bulls were getting sick of my attitude. Cartwright was upfront with me about that.

"Do you want to be here?" he asked.

"Yes, I do."

"You have to relax because I don't want them to trade you."

The idea of being traded surprised me. It was the first time I had thought about not being a Chicago Bull. I took that personally.

"You're a big part of this team," he told me. "You can be a great player, but you can't be acting out. Just relax and try to play the game."

"I'll work on it. I'll be better."

Despite what I told him, I didn't understand the process of getting better or what it would take for us to become a good team. Today I understand that it takes time, but in my head I didn't have that time. I wanted to be good right now. I wanted to win right now. I wanted to be a scorer right now. When that didn't happen it only made things worse. I was willing to work, but I wasn't willing to wait. I didn't know how to handle that frustration.

Even though Bill had made it clear I was nearing my last chance with the Bulls, things didn't change. I don't know if I got a technical foul or got in someone's face the next game, but it seemed pretty clear that I couldn't control my emotions. We had lost several games in a row before we were scheduled to play at Miami on February 18. It was also a couple days before the trade deadline. The team was on the bus to the arena in Miami when Bill Cartwright sat down next to me.

"They made the decision to trade you," he said.

"What? Where?"

He explained that Brad Miller, Ron Mercer, Kevin Ollie, and I were going to Indiana. Jalen Rose, Travis Best, Norm Richardson, and a second-round draft pick were coming back to Chicago.

"You don't have to get dressed tonight," Cartwright said.

I guess it wasn't a surprise. He told me it could happen. He even told me why. But it's still hard to hear those words come out of your coach's mouth. I took it personally. It wasn't until I got older that I realized that the NBA is just a business. Any player can be traded at any time. You don't have to be detrimental to the team or playing bad to get traded. You can be traded because you're a good commodity or your salary works under the salary cap. It's a business, but I took it personally.

I didn't want to go out like that. Spend my last game as a Bull sitting on the bench in my suit? Hell no. Fuck that. The Bulls were my favorite team growing up and I wanted to go out there in that uniform one last time. I got dressed and went out on the court to shoot. I enjoyed that one last moment as a Bull. Of course, they got mad at me for that because I wasn't supposed to be shooting, but I didn't care. I went back in the locker room to change into my street clothes so I could sit on the bench for the game, but I made sure to wear my Bulls jersey under my suit.

When I got back to Chicago, I had a meeting with Jerry Krause in his office. I had a lot of conversations with Jerry during my time in Chicago. We met a couple of times to discuss my attitude. On multiple occasions I tried to tell him that I was frustrated because I kept missing shots and couldn't score like I wanted to. He always told me the same thing.

"I'm not worried about that. Any great defender like you can score the ball. It's only a matter of time," he said.

I guess that never sank in with me, which is probably why I got traded.

This time our conversation was a little different. It was the last one we were probably going to have so I didn't say much. I just sat there and listened.

"We really wish you could have stayed here, Ron," Krause said.

"I understand," I said, even though I really didn't.

"We had a good time here. You were a good player for us and you'll continue to be a good player. Indiana is a great organization. Donnie Walsh is a great GM and a good person."

He wished me the best of luck. We shook hands and that was it. On my way out of the building I saw a picture of me hanging on the wall. *They won't be needing this anymore.* I ripped the picture right off the wall and continued out to my car.

I left Chicago on a bad note. I admit that I was a train wreck waiting to happen. It wouldn't have mattered what team I was on at that point in my career. I could have been on the Lakers and they probably would have traded me, too. I was out of control. If I could go back and mentor my younger self, I'd make sure that I had more fun playing basketball. Sometimes it's easy to forget that this is all just a game. Relax and have a good time. Sometimes that's what's most important. If you can do that, everything else will fall into place.

INDIANA

Chapter 12

Naptown

I started the 2001–02 season with the Bulls, but I finished it with the Pacers.

That transition wasn't as difficult as I thought it was going to be. The Pacers were led by Reggie Miller and Jermaine O'Neal. The coach was former Pistons legend Isiah Thomas. The whole team was welcoming and Isiah went out of his way to make me feel like he wanted me there. Everyone helped me out when I got to Indiana so it didn't take me long to fit in.

Things moved so quickly. Before I could wrap my head around being traded by the Bulls, I was in the starting lineup for my first game with the Pacers. I was also in the middle of a race to get into the playoffs. From the day I was drafted, all I ever wanted to do was win a championship. I didn't have the offensive skills at the time to lead my team and Chicago was never in contention. At the time of the trade, the Pacers were in 10th place in the Eastern Conference, but only a half game out of the eighth and final playoff spot. That was all I thought about. It was more comfortable territory for me and made the season interesting. The race came right down to the wire. We won the last five games of the season and snuck into the playoffs as the eighth seed, just one game ahead of the Milwaukee Bucks.

That meant a matchup with the New Jersey Nets in the first round, who were the top seed. They had Jason Kidd, Kenyon Martin, Kerry Kittles, and Richard Jefferson. They were expected to beat us, but we carried the momentum of that five-game winning streak into the playoffs and won the first game of that five-game series. It was a back-and-forth game, but we pulled ahead at the end. Jermaine scored 30 points. He was only a year older than me, but he had more experience because he had entered the NBA right out of high school. It had taken some time but he was starting to come into his own and was a presence in the post.

For me, the playoffs were no different than the regular season. Yes, the game was faster and more intense, but I expected that going in. That's how I practiced, so when we made it to the playoffs it felt like I was right where I wanted to be. I was playing well until I hurt my ankle in Game 2. I didn't miss any time, but I was limited in what I could do.

I also got my first taste of what Reggie Miller could do on the court during that series. Game 5 was a double-overtime classic in New Jersey. Reggie was amazing. He banked in a shot from about 40 feet out at the buzzer to send the game into overtime. Reggie didn't quit when we were down and hit some very big shots. He then had a huge dunk to tie the game and force a second overtime. He was so clutch, but we didn't step up as a team and fell apart in the second OT. Jason Kidd took over and helped the Nets clinch the series with a 120–109 win.

The Nets went on to the NBA Finals that year, where they were swept by the Lakers. That was the team with Kobe and Shaquille O'Neal that won the title for the third time in a row. My first trip to the NBA playoffs was over in five games. There was so much buildup and anticipation only for it to be over much too quickly. It reminded me of my freshman year at St. John's. The difference with that Pacers team was that we were the eighth seed. We overachieved. We had a good run and we knew we'd be back. The season was over, but there was a good feeling surrounding that team. It was a feeling that I hadn't experienced in a long time.

Reggie was the leader of that team and I knew he wanted a championship before he retired. He could be vocal when he had to, but Reggie led by example. He kept things positive and was the guy in the locker room always reminding us about how good we could be. He didn't have to get in people's faces or get angry. We saw how hard he worked and how much he cared about the game, and we knew we had to follow his lead. Reggie was a workaholic. If we had a game at 7:00 at night, he would get to the gym at 4:00 in the afternoon. He was the first one at practice and the last to leave. And while he was there, he took a lot of shots. He was very impressive.

It was a different atmosphere in Indiana. That was a place where I could have learned a lot, but I wasn't the best listener and I wasn't always open to criticism. I didn't truly appreciate the opportunity that had fallen into my lap because of the trade. Not only was I playing with a future Hall of Famer in Reggie Miller, but we had a Hall of Famer as a coach in Isiah. He could get me to focus and keep me in check. A few years later, another Hall of Famer, Larry Bird, was named the director of basketball operations. Those were all NBA legends. They were some of the best players in the history of the game. They all reached out and tried to help me with my own game.

My first setback came that summer when I went in for a physical. They did an EKG; a simple and painless test that records your heartbeat. When the results came in, the doctor sat me down and explained that I had a heart murmur. It wasn't a major problem now, but it could be life-threatening down the road. My heart could fail me if I didn't take care of it. It required surgery to seal a hole between my aorta and pulmonary artery.

In a way, I shouldn't have been completely surprised. I always got tired easily playing ball, even back in college. That might have had something to do with partying too much and staying out late, but even in the NBA I still got tired. I would fight through it but no matter how much I worked on my conditioning, I'd always be tired in the fourth quarter. The doctors told me that my heart murmur might have had something to do with that, so in July of 2002 I decided to have the surgery.

At the time, I was more concerned about having to sit out some games than I was my long-term health, so the day after the procedure I showed up at the Pacers facility. I wasn't looking to play full court or anything like that. I wasn't even going to run. I just wanted to shoot some free throws, but even doing that I could feel my heart beating like it was going to pop out of my chest. I had to sit down for a while and I decided to take the rest of the day off before I did some real damage. I came back the next day to shoot and everything felt fine. Pretty soon, I was back to normal.

In fact, I was better than back to normal. I wasn't getting tired on the court anymore. My production went up. My offensive game improved. I think the surgery had a lot to do with that. I was able to play better in the fourth quarter because I felt better. I had more energy.

Unfortunately, I didn't always channel that energy into something positive during my second season with the Pacers. I may have been playing better, but I was at the center of more controversy. That season I led the league in flagrant fouls. I must have led the league in fines and suspensions too, because it felt like I constantly had to sit out. Prior to that season, I had only been suspended once. It happened during the 2001 season with the Bulls, when I got into a scuffle with Glenn Robinson of the Bucks.

My problems in Indiana started in December of 2002 during a confrontation with Raja Bell, who was with the Dallas Mavericks at the time. The next month, I broke a camera at Madison Square Garden after a loss to the Knicks. A few weeks later, we were in Miami when Caron Butler and I exchanged hard fouls. Pat Riley got involved, and I brushed him accidentally. I wasn't trying to bump him, but he thought I was and pushed me away. I later gave the fans the finger. I was suspended for that.

The NBA gives out automatic suspensions once you've collected a certain number of flagrant or technical fouls. That policy started to catch up with me in March. I gave the fans in Cleveland the finger after another altercation in April. By that point, I had been suspended five times and missed a total of 12 games. I was fined $175,000 and lost more than $250,000 in salary. And the season wasn't even over yet.

My behavior was borne out of my attitude back then, which was not to let anybody shove me around. Nobody intimidated me. When people would come at me, I would go back at them. I respected a lot of players but nobody intimidated me. When the game got heated, I would get more intense. I would bump people and play tougher defense. I went out there trying to eat people alive and push things to the absolute limit. When I was on my game, it felt like I could stop anybody.

My problem was that I took things too far. There were times when I deserved to be fined and I deserved to be suspended. I shouldn't have been doing what I was doing. I didn't need to be out there breaking cameras and giving fans the finger. I set myself up for disaster. I had developed a reputation around the league: players, coaches, and fans thought of me as a guy who would easily lose his cool. The refs were just waiting for me to step out of line, so guys on the other team would try to rile me up to get a reaction. I'd give it to them and step right into the trap. Every fine and suspension only drew more attention to my behavior and gave me a shorter leash with the refs. Meanwhile, the fines and suspensions fueled my fire and got me more upset, making it more likely that I'd act out in the heat of the moment. It became a vicious circle and a pattern that I couldn't seem to break.

My teammates had every right to get frustrated with me. During one game, Jermaine actually pulled me to the side of the court and said, "You gotta stop doing this bullshit if you wanna win." He didn't baby me and told it to me like it was. Jermaine was more mature and he was proving that he was a great leader of that team.

Reggie Miller took a different approach. He pulled me off to the side a couple different times that season, too. We had some good talks. He was always trying to get me to calm down and relax. He knew I was going through some shit and he was always patient with me. The thing that I came to respect about Reggie the most was that he never judged me or got down on me for being the unstable teammate that I was for a long time. He was supportive. As I got older, I learned to take a page from Reggie's book.

Everyone on that team had my back but I didn't always take their advice to heart. I was my own worst enemy and I was to blame for many of my problems. That said, it's not like I was the first hard-nosed player in the league. When I was younger, I learned by watching teams like the Knicks and the Pistons. I saw players like Bill Laimbeer and Dennis Rodman do the same exact thing I was doing. They were tough. They played hard. They played with passion. All of us did whatever it took to win. Some people were starting to call me a dirty player, but I never played dirty. I never went out there trying to hurt people. I lost my temper and did foolish things when I was caught up in the moment. I didn't always do the right thing but that's not the same as being dirty.

What bothered me the most was that I knew there were kids out there watching me, just as I had watched Laimbeer and Rodman when I was a kid. I didn't want anybody seeing my behavior on the court and thinking it was okay to act like that. I wouldn't want my son to look up to a player, or wear the jersey of a player, who was getting into trouble the way I was. I wanted my kids looking up to the good people, and more than anything else, that made me want to change my on-court behavior.

In spite of all of those problems and distractions, we had improved tremendously as a team. We finished the season with a 48–34 record, which earned us the third seed in the Eastern Conference playoffs. That set up a matchup with the sixth-seeded Boston Celtics. With home-court advantage, we were definitely favored to win.

That series was one of the first of many playoff battles I would have with Paul Pierce. He came out in Game 1 ready to play and busted my ass. He dropped 40 in that first game, including 21-of-21 from the foul line, an NBA playoff record. He brought the Celtics back from 13 down with about seven and a half minutes left to win that game. I fouled out trying to guard him. We didn't get off to the start we wanted to.

I came back determined in Game 2 to lock up Pierce. We won that one 89–77 but Boston took three of the next four, including a 20-point win on their home court in Game 6. I was mad at our team because I didn't feel that everybody was working as hard as they could. I always took that personally. Yeah, we made it to the playoffs, but for the second year in a row we were out in the first round.

Watching the Celtics celebrate a win on their own court was an awful feeling. It was not a good way to end a season. I needed to get off that court but as I was headed to the tunnel, something hit me in the head. I looked to the ground but the floor was a mess. I couldn't see what it was, but it was heavy and I could tell exactly where it came from. I spun around and spotted the guy who threw it immediately. I could just tell it was him. We were looking right at each other. That was the absolute worst time he could have chosen to hit me with something.

I took a step toward the crowd but I was being held back. It was Mel Daniels. Mel was an all-time Pacers great who was then the director of player personnel. He saw what happened and knew exactly what I was thinking.

"Easy, now. Just forget about it," Mel said.

But I wasn't listening. I wanted to get up into the stands.

"No fucking way," I told him.

I pushed Mel but he was strong enough to hold me back and get me into the locker room.

Mel did the right thing that day and I have him to thank for not allowing that situation to escalate. At the time, I had no idea how disastrous that confrontation could have turned out. It was a sign of things to come, but I wasn't able to recognize any of those warning signs. I was a bomb waiting to explode. It was only a matter of time.

Chapter 13

From Pretenders to Contenders

Losing in the first round in back-to-back years was horrible but I loved living in Indiana.

I bought a house out in the suburbs. I don't know what it was about the suburbs, but people let you be yourself out there. I got along with all my neighbors. Everyone was so laid-back. I had one neighbor named Dorothy. She was in her seventies and used to invite me over to eat pie and listen to country music. I'd take her up on that offer every time to get myself some pie and just listen to her tell stories.

I wasn't living there long before Indiana felt like home to me, which was strange because it was the complete opposite of what I was used to. I had lived in New York and then Chicago my entire life. I loved Indiana so much that I even convinced my mom to move out of Queens and bought her a house right around the block. She never wanted to leave the hood, even after I was drafted and wanted to buy her a house, but I sold her on Indiana. I loved it and wanted to spend the rest of my life there.

There weren't any distractions that off-season and I took full advantage of the peace and quiet. I spent most of my time working out. I got to the gym at 9:00 AM and worked out with our strength coach, Bill Dean. I then worked out with Chuck Person, who was working in the Pacers front office then, at 10:00. At 10:45, we played full court. After lunch, I went over to the Jewish Community Center to lift and swim. That was my day. At night, I'd take my kids to some WNBA games. I really got into the Indiana Fever.

There were some big changes in my personal life that summer, too. I broke up with Jenny, and she moved back to New York with Jeron. We had some rough times but we're on good terms now. In the meantime, I had gotten back together with Kimsha. When we first met, I knew I wanted to spend the rest of my life with her. She was a good girl and a sweetheart, and she always had my best interests in mind. She was also a fighter and never let me settle for less. She has always been right when offering advice on friends or letting me know when I fucked up. We spent a lot of time apart and had our differences, but when it came to the things that were really important, we saw eye to eye. We were married that June and Kimsha gave birth to our daughter Diamond soon after. I was a 23-year-old father of four.

My life kept changing and so did the team. In the summer of 2003 the Pacers hired Larry Bird as the director of basketball operations. One of the first things Larry did was fire head coach Isiah Thomas and replace him with Rick Carlisle. Rick had coached the Pistons and was an assistant under Larry a few years earlier when Larry was the head coach in Indiana.

Carlisle also played with Bird on the Celtics in the 1980s, so they went way back.

I had never met Rick before so it took a little while for us to get on the same page, but once we did we understood each other. Rick and I got along well. More than anything, Rick was an incredibly smart basketball coach. He controlled everything that happened on the court. That was frustrating for the players who wanted to go out there and do their own thing, because Rick would call the play every single trip down the court. It took us a long time to get used to his style, but we were winning so we went along.

There are not many coaches, if any at all, who can coach the way Rick does. The reason it worked so well for him was because he could tell immediately when something wasn't right. He knew when to let go or when to hold back. It's hard to consistently pick the right play while making sure everyone is involved and that the team respects you. And everyone on that team had a lot of respect for Rick. He would call us out when we were wrong, but Rick had our backs and looked out for us. All of those things had to happen for that style of coaching to be successful, but Rick made it work. He's still making it work to this day.

Those practices we had were real battles. We went at it. One day, Mike Brown, one of Rick's assistants at the time, was leading the scrimmages. He wanted the first team to go up against the second team. I thought it was a stupid idea and I let him know it.

"Go out and beat them. Prove that you're better," he said.

So, we played the game. The second unit beat the starters, and it wasn't like we weren't trying. I couldn't believe it. I was furious.

"Start running," Mike said.

I felt like he was rubbing it in, so I punted the ball into the bleachers. But Mike wouldn't let me off the hook. He called me out.

"Go get it," he said.

"No. I'm not getting it."

For a second it looked like we might go at it, but I knew better than to confront a coach that way. I was frustrated but Mike was right to challenge me when I did something wrong. He didn't let me get away with anything, and even though I didn't always listen to him when I should have, I really came to respect Mike Brown because of that. I ended up running that day, too.

I had my fiery moments, but overall I did not have as many on-court incidents that year. I sat out a game in March for an altercation with Portland's Derek Anderson, but when it came to suspensions, fines, and flagrant fouls, I mostly stayed out of trouble. It might have been because I was married and maturing with age, but I think part of it had to do with Rick. He kept us focused on what was really important. We knew our team had a chance to win the title and I didn't want to jeopardize that. That season I made a conscious decision to focus on basketball and not to cross the line when I didn't need to.

It paid off. I made my first All-Star team that season, as Jermaine and I both represented the Eastern Conference in the 2004 All-Star Game, in Los Angeles. Jermaine started but I came off the bench. I was upset because I felt that I was the best small forward in the league and playing on the best team in the league. But I tried to go out and have fun. It was a good time but I was not on the court at the end of the game. That was something else I really wanted, but it made me realize that nobody was taking the Indiana Pacers seriously. That lit a fire under me that stayed lit for the rest of the season.

I had a minor setback in February when I had to have thumb surgery. I was supposed to sit out a month, but I only missed five games and was back in the lineup by early March. We finished the year strong and with the best record in the NBA, at 61–21. We were the top seed in the East going into the playoffs.

Rick was pushing Jermaine for MVP that year. I thought I had an MVP year as well. That wasn't a reach if you looked at what I was doing on both sides of the ball, but the league never valued defense the same way it does offense. The award went to Minnesota's Kevin Garnett that year, even though we were the team with the best record. Indiana was a small market so we didn't get the attention that a team like the Lakers would have gotten if they finished with the best record. It felt like we were flying under the radar.

I might not have been getting any credit for my offense, but the league did recognize my defense. On April 19 I learned that I had won the Defensive Player of the Year award. I beat out Detroit's Ben Wallace, who had won the award the previous two seasons. San Antonio Spurs coach Gregg Popovich came out and said the Spurs' Bruce Bowen should have won it. Popovich was mad because Rick Carlisle did a lot of campaigning for me. Bruce was a great defensive player, but I felt that I had one of the best years defensively that the NBA had ever seen. I held Kobe Bryant and Tracy McGrady well below their averages when I guarded them— Rick's campaigning had nothing to do with that.

Popovich's comments took some of the fun out of the award for me. I didn't want it to be in question, so I told the media that I would play Bruce Bowen in a game of one-on-one for the award. I understood where Popovich was coming from—he was supporting his player—but at the end of the day

I was named to the NBA All-Defensive team by the coaches and had the most first-place votes.

That season I guarded every team's best player and I held them to eight points a game, on nine shots. I always prided myself on my defense. It's what got me so far. I used to cut out pictures of the players I had to guard and post them in my locker. It was something I thought about all the time. Back in high school, I felt that I never got the respect I deserved when I shut down some of the best players in the country. It felt like nobody noticed or cared. After winning Defensive Player of the Year in the NBA, it felt like people finally took notice. I was always told that I was a great defender, but to be acknowledged for it by the league was an incredible feeling.

Winning the award was also humbling. I beat out a lot of great defenders that year including Wallace, Bowen, Lindsey Hunter, and Shaq. To see my name mentioned among some of the legends who previously won the award was unbelievable. I was suddenly in the same category as Dikembe Mutombo, Alonzo Mourning, Gary Payton, Hakeem Olajuwon, David Robinson, and Dennis Rodman, to name a few. A lot of people forget that it was Rodman who helped Jordan win three of those rings. Rodman was the man back in the day. I enjoyed watching him play and he did a lot of good for the NBA by putting the spotlight on defense and rebounding. It was nice to see a guy getting respect for doing something other than scoring. I loved his game and his basketball mind. When I was coming up in the league, MJ was also proving that he was one of the best defensive players in the NBA. Even after I broke his ribs in that pickup game, Jordan gave me a lot of publicity for being a good defensive player and I have to thank him for that. I was proud to be acknowledged by him and included in the conversation with all those great defensive players.

I didn't have time to get too excited about the award because we still had the playoffs to focus on. That was what mattered. I would have traded five Defensive Player of the Year awards for one championship ring. That was always the goal and we had a very good chance that year. We also had Reggie Miller. Reggie's numbers were down from his prime years, but he was still Reggie Miller.

We drew the Celtics in the first round for the second year in a row. I was so excited for that series, because of how things went down the previous year. I wanted another chance to go up against Paul Pierce and redeem myself. He got the better of us last time, but that wasn't going to happen again. Since I was the one guarding Pierce, I put a lot of the blame for that loss on my shoulders. The Celtics may have been the No. 8 seed and we were heavily favored, but we did not overlook that team.

We won the first game 104–88, but it wasn't all good news. I was on the bench at one point when I saw Brandon Hunter of the Celtics toss Jermaine to the floor. I could see Jermaine was about to lose his cool, so I jumped up and came to his defense. I didn't actually make it all the way out there—I came back to the bench before anything happened—but the NBA had a rule that any player who left the bench would be suspended for a game. I may not have liked the rule, but I had to abide by it. I was suspended for Game 2 but luckily the team didn't need me. Al Harrington and Jonathan Bender stepped up and we won again, this time by 13. Al played great for us that year. He could have easily been Sixth Man of the Year.

We not only swept the Celtics that year, but we won all of our games by double figures. Pierce scored some points, but he didn't hurt us like he did the year before and shot only 34 percent from the field. That would not be my last series against Paul. He was a competitor. Those games were battles.

We went at it and he was not an easy cover, but I made sure to hound him when I was in the game. That series it was Paul who lost his cool and got frustrated: in the first quarter of Game 4 he got a tech for pushing me to the floor.

We were supposed to beat the Celtics, so our sweep wasn't a big deal to the rest of the league. But it meant a lot to us and it meant a lot to me. That was the first time I had made it past the opening round of the playoffs in my career.

We had to wait 11 days to start our second-round series against the Heat. That was a long-ass time. Leaders like Reggie did a good job of keeping us grounded during the season, and in the playoffs he kept us on track. When we were tied 2–2 with the Heat and facing adversity for the very first time all season, Reggie didn't allow us to panic. He kept it simple: "What went wrong and how do we fix it?" We corrected our mistakes. We won the series and advanced to the Eastern Conference Finals against the Pistons.

Every game against the Pistons was intense. It was an old-school rivalry—those games were some of the toughest and most physical I would ever play in my career. It was hard to come down after those games because I would get so wound up. Even when we won, I would walk out of the arena angry after playing the Pistons. We hated each other. We looked at that series like it was the NBA Finals. We thought that whoever won that series would beat whoever came out of the West. Defense wins championships and we were the two best defensive teams in the league.

Jermaine and Jamaal Tinsley were playing hurt, but Reggie Miller reminded everyone why he was a future Hall of Famer. Game 1 was close all the way to the end. Reggie wasn't scoring. He didn't have a field goal the entire game, but with 30 seconds left he hit a three to give us the lead. It was his only basket of the game but it was the basket that won it for us. Reggie was a player who could put up big numbers, but it wasn't just about putting up big numbers. It was about doing whatever it took to win. Even a scorer like Reggie Miller knew when to pull back and when to step up.

I didn't have a good series. I couldn't hit a damn shot. I never got it together. We weren't playing well as a team. We found ourselves down 3–2 facing a Game 6 in Detroit.

With four minutes left, the Pistons had the ball. I was guarding Richard Hamilton, and as he backed into me he hit me in the stomach and knocked me off balance. I put my arm up to stop him from setting up where he wanted to, but it caught him right in the face. He went down hard. He was already wearing that face mask, the one he wore for the rest of his career, because he had broken his nose twice that year. It looked worse than it was. Everyone called it a dirty play, but I wasn't trying to elbow him in the face like that. Those things just happen when you have two people fighting for position, but I knew I caught him bad right away. That's why I raised my hand. I still got slapped with a flagrant. Hamilton hit his foul shots and the Pistons took the lead for the first time. Because of the flagrant foul, they got the ball right back and Rasheed Wallace got a huge dunk. The fans were on their feet. That was a big swing for the Pistons and they won the game 69–65. Series over.

That series only intensified our rivalry with the Pistons, who went on to win the NBA championship that year by beating a Lakers team with four future Hall of Famers. That Pistons team of Chauncey Billups, Ben Wallace, Rasheed Wallace, Rip Hamilton, and Tayshawn Prince was the only team in NBA history to win a championship without a player who ever made First Team All-NBA. They were a team without a big star. They did it because they played better defense. They may not have had better individual players, but those individual players played better together as a team. We couldn't wait to get a piece of the Pistons the next season.

Every year I like to think I improved as a player, but the summer before the 2004 season was when I felt I made the most progress. I was becoming a better scorer, and one of the people responsible for that was Larry Bird. Larry coached me up in the summer. He may have been in the front office, but he'd still come down to the court to work me out. That helped me so much. He'd be down there every day, along with Chuck Person, and together they made sure I got better.

I had never been the best athlete. There were always guys in the league who could run faster and jump higher. I got where I was because I hustled and I tried to work harder than everyone else. I felt limited as an offensive player, and my lack of athletic ability had something to do with that. Larry Bird was not a gifted athlete either, but he was still a tremendous scorer. I had Larry working with me so I straight-up asked him: "How did you always get to the basket?"

"You have to be able to shoot," he told me. "Once you can prove that you can make a jump shot, they have to come out and guard you. That opens up the defense and gives you more options. Then, just take what they give you."

"That's it?"

"If the defense gives you a lane, take it. If they give you an open shot, take it."

It sounded so simple, but it made sense. I thought back to a play in Game 6 against Detroit when I drove passed Tayshaun Prince. He hit the ground, but I got called for the offensive foul. I was 260 pounds. What was I supposed to do in that situation? It felt like the referees always favored the smaller players. There was also a lot of flopping. I never played defense like that, but it was the way the game had evolved. That limited what I could do on offense, but if players didn't want to get up in my face and lock me up, then they were basically giving me an open jump shot.

I didn't miss a chance to learn from Larry Bird and I credit him with making me a better offensive player. Sometimes it would be just me and him down in the gym. I worked on my shot, I took his advice, and I got better. Once I could consistently hit a midrange jump shot, my offensive game had dimension. It freed me up to drive to the basket because guys couldn't always play off me. When I started taking what the defense gave me, my scoring average went up.

I learned a lot during those summers with Larry, but I didn't fully appreciate what he was doing for me. I feel bad about that now, because I feel like I took his time for granted. He didn't need to be down there on the court helping me out, but he was. I messed up a lot of the opportunities I had there in Indiana. The Pacers gave me so much and they deserved more in return.

Chapter 14

The Malice at the Palace

Losing to the Pistons in the 2003–04 Eastern Conference Finals stung.

At the beginning of the 2004–05 season, we set out to prove that the Pacers were the best team in the league. I dropped 31 in the opener against Cleveland and was averaging 24 points per game in the early part of the season. Things were finally coming together. I finally felt like I could take over an NBA game and score when I had to. I was even comfortable stepping behind the line and shooting threes. I was becoming a more complete player.

I had just won Defensive Player of the Year, but I wanted to win Defensive Player of the Year and MVP that year. I also had my sights set on the scoring title. That may sound selfish, but my motivation wasn't selfish. Winning a championship was still the priority, but winning the scoring title and MVP was my own personal goal. That gave me something to shoot for. It pushed me and motivated me to improve. I wanted to take 20 points away from the other team's best player and then put up 20 of my own.

We picked up Stephen Jackson during the off-season in a trade for Al Harrington. Stephen was another tough player who worked hard. He had a good relationship with Mike Brown, who coached Stephen back in San Antonio, where they won an NBA championship together in 2003. Stephen knew what it took to be a champion. We shared the same passion and the same intensity, so we worked well together. We had some battles in practice and he was not scared of getting into it with anybody. He helped bring intensity to that team.

I spent the majority of my spare time working on music. I started my own record label, called Tru Warier, and planned on releasing my own album soon. I may have been working a little too much on my music. The group Allure was signed to my label and I spent the summer on tour helping them promote their album, which was due out at the end of November. I was doing all that while also trying to work out.

My life off the court had become stressful. I was arguing more with Kimsha. I wanted to be married, but I clearly wasn't ready to be married at that time. All of that pressure and stress was magnified when my Grandma Hattie passed away in October. She was my mother's mother and we were close growing up, so that was difficult for me. Even though I was playing well, I was worn down mentally and physically. Worse, I was distracted and the season was only just starting.

My head was not in a good place so I asked Rick Carlisle if I could take some time off. My request came off the wrong way, to say the least. I had no right to ask for that time off, but looking back I really needed it. I was lost and still trying to figure out who I was as a person and where I was going. Some of my teammates thought it was funny that I actually asked for time off, but the organization didn't think it was that funny. Rick said I compromised the integrity of the team but didn't go into detail when speaking to the media. I sat for two games. It wasn't the break that I was looking for, but it was all I was going to get. We moved past it and focused on winning a championship together.

In spite of my own personal distractions, everything was on point for us as a team that year, right up until November, 19, 2004. It was Pacers versus Pistons at the Palace of Auburn Hills. I had just turned 25 years old a few days earlier. The Pistons were the defending NBA champions and now we had a chance to prove it was our turn. That was also a nationally televised game on ESPN and the network had been hyping it all week.

We didn't have everyone in the lineup. Reggie Miller, Anthony Johnson, and Scot Pollard all sat out. There was talk Detroit's Ben Wallace wasn't going to play. He had missed two games because his brother had passed away from brain cancer, but we learned that he was going to be in the lineup. It would be his first game back.

When I stepped onto the court for shootaround, I saw that the fans had all kinds of signs that said things like, RON ARTEST IS CRAZY and RON ARTEST NEEDS ZOLOFT. I went over and was joking with some of them, but it was all business once the game started.

We jumped out to a quick lead. I dropped 17 in the first quarter. We were up as many as 20 before going into the locker room up by 16 at halftime. But the Pistons didn't quit. All of our games against the Pistons were physical, but that one was particularly brutal.

Things got heated toward the end. In the fourth quarter, Rip Hamilton elbowed Jamaal Tinsley in the back on his way up the court and got called for a flagrant foul. It felt like payback for the elbow I gave Rip the previous season.

The Pistons inched back but Stephen Jackson and Jermaine O'Neal helped us pull ahead. The Pistons missed about 10 in a row which just about put the game out of reach. With 90 seconds left, I caught the ball in the middle of the key. I went up for a layup when Ben Wallace fouled me from behind and knocked me into the base of the basket. No foul was called. It didn't matter, because the game was as good as over. We were up 97–82 with 45 seconds left.

Stephen Jackson was guarding Ben Wallace when Ben got the ball in the post. Stephen let him go across the key. I didn't care what the score was. I was going to foul him. We had been battling all game. I wasn't about to let him get an easy bucket. I never give up easy buckets. I went after the ball and gave him a hard foul, but nothing more. I certainly didn't try to hurt him. The ref blew the whistle and the play was over, but Ben charged at me and shoved me in the face with both hands.

I did not expect him to react that way. I didn't want to fight. I was playing well and had endorsements lined up. I didn't want to ruin any of that so I backed away. But he kept coming at me. Both benches were up and people were trying to keep us separated. I didn't want to escalate the fight. I had been told to get myself out of those situations when they came up, so that's exactly what I tried to do.

A lot of people felt that neither of us should've been in the game at that point, but we had a short bench and Pistons coach Larry Brown later said that he didn't want to embarrass any of his bench players by putting them in for the last 45 seconds. Some of the blame could also be put on the refs, because the fouls were getting harder and harder as that game went on. Things were slowly getting out of control toward the end.

Rasheed Wallace actually helped the rest of the guys on the Pistons back off. I wanted to get away from everyone so I lied down on the scorer's table. I put on the headset to play the whole thing off as a joke. I wanted to lighten the mood and show that I wasn't bothered by it. Reggie Miller was in his street clothes, but he came over and patted me on the chest to calm me down. But I was calm. I was fine. I was under control. I didn't engage. I did everything possible to avoid a confrontation. I felt that my role in the altercation was over.

Some of the other guys were still saying shit and standing toe-to-toe. Stephen Jackson and Rip, who were friends, looked like they were going to throw blows. Coaches and players for both teams were out on the court. Ben was still upset. He kept trying to get closer to me and come at me. He even threw an armband at me. I don't know why the refs didn't throw him out of the game. It's so easy to look back and think of all the things our team, the Pistons, the refs, and certain fans could have done that would have prevented the brawl, but emotions were high and everything happened so fast.

On TV, they were talking about who was going to get ejected. My name wasn't being mentioned in that conversation yet. While I was lying on the scorer's table, one of the guys in the press row said to me, "Ron, don't go anywhere. I wanna talk to you at the end of the game."

That's when my life changed.

A blue plastic cup of Diet Coke came flying from the stands. It bounced off my chest and hit me in the face.

I had never experienced that before. I was prepared for anything that could happen on the court, but as soon as I was hit in the face with that cup, this became an off-the-court incident.

I honestly don't remember the next few seconds.

What I do remember was being up in the stands going after the guy who I thought had thrown the cup. I closed in on him and started to shake him. I didn't hit him. I just kept yelling, "Did you do it? Did you throw that?"

"No, man! No!" he kept saying.

It turned out he was right. I didn't know it at the time, but the guy I went after, Michael Ryan, didn't throw the cup. It was the guy standing right next to him, John Green. Seconds earlier, Ryan and Green had made a bet that Green couldn't hit me with the cup of Diet Coke. When I ran up into the stands, I saw Ryan with his hand in the air and assumed that he was the one who threw the cup, but he was just responding to what Green had done. As I went after Ryan, it was Green who grabbed me from behind.

I was getting pulled in every direction when I got hit with another drink. Stephen Jackson, who had followed me into the crowd, went after that guy. A bunch of my teammates rushed into the stands to grab me and I saw them getting pummeled by fans. I later found out that Ben Wallace's brother David was in the stands watching the game and threw a punch at my teammate Fred Jones. Reggie and Chuck Person had jumped in and were trying to get me out of there. On my way back down to the court, I got punched by another fan from behind. I turned around and started swinging. More drinks were thrown. I was in pure survival mode at that point.

I finally made it out of the stands and back onto the court only to have two more fans come right up to me. I punched one of the guys—A.J. Shackleford. He went down and brought his friend, Charlie Haddad, to the floor with him. I don't know what that guy was thinking coming down onto the court like that. That was dumb. I was actually trying to hit him again, but I couldn't come back with the left and give him that two-piece because I slipped on all the soda, beer, and ice that had spilled all over the floor. It was a mess. Jermaine then came running in from the side. He threw a punch at Haddad, but Jermaine slipped and the punch grazed the side of Haddad's head. We later learned that Haddad had a long history of incidents at the Palace, and once threatened to pour a drink on

Yao Ming's head. He had already been confronted by security earlier in the night before the brawl.

It was William Wesley, who had been sitting courtside that night, who finally pulled me away. In the middle of all the chaos, a police officer came running up to us with his mace out. He was getting ready to spray me in the face. Reggie put an arm out to stop him and yelled, "No, no, no, we got him!"

I just wanted to get off that court and out of that arena as quickly as possible, but to get to the tunnel we had to walk between two rows of fans. I thought we might have to fight our way out of the arena. It felt like every single person there was out to get us. Those were average everyday people who probably led normal lives, but they had gone crazy that night. They weren't just throwing plastic cups. They were throwing change and full water bottles. Chuck Person was covering my face because people were throwing so much shit. Jermaine almost got hit with a goddamn chair. We literally had to push our way through. No security was there to help us or anything. There was no way we were going to play the final 45 seconds after that. The refs eventually called the game and we won, but that didn't matter anymore.

We made it to the locker room and I sat down with Stephen Jackson and Jamaal Tinsley. The magnitude of what just happened hadn't sunk in yet. I knew it was bad, but a part of me hoped that it wasn't. Wanting some kind of confirmation that things could still turn out okay, I asked, "Do you think we're gonna get in trouble?" Stephen lost it. He looked at me like I was nuts.

"I don't think we're even gonna have a job," he said.

The nerves and the energy in the room were so high that Jermaine got into a shouting match with Rick Carlisle. Now there was tension between the players and the coaches. Everyone had bruises and cuts. I learned later that I accidentally hurt Pacers radio play-by-play announcer Mark Boyle. I don't even remember seeing him, but apparently he tried to stop me from going into the stands. I went right over him and broke five vertebrate in his back. I felt awful.

The cops were looking to arrest me. I heard they tried to take Jermaine and Mike Brown in, but Jermaine said no. He wasn't going to go with any cops after what happened. Luckily, assistant coach Kevin O'Neill got me on the bus. He wouldn't let the cops come near me. In the end, the police actually helped us get to the bus and get out of there.

The security was great in the NBA, but they weren't prepared for something like that. There were not enough police officers in the arena that night. They had old ladies working as ushers who were just trying to pay their bills. They couldn't stop a fight. Nobody saw it coming. Nobody knew that some dumbass motherfucker from the stands was going to throw something onto the court. Most of the fans are great. Some are obnoxious, but I'd say 99 percent of them are good people who don't cause any problems. I got nothing against Detroit or the fans, but the Palace was gangster like that. I don't know of any other fans in any other city that would have done what they did that night.

The NBA doubled security the very next game and security is much better these days. They have a lot of "Ron Artest rules" in the NBA now. Fans have to walk through metal detectors to get into the arena. If players on the bench go two feet onto the court, suspensions are handed down. They even limit the size and number of alcoholic beverages you can buy in an arena.

I was a big name in the league. I played for an important franchise. We were a title contender and it was a game against the reigning NBA champs. It was a big deal. That game went horribly wrong, and unfortunately one of the reasons it escalated was directly related to my decision to go into the stands. Everything happened so fast. I was just reacting without thinking, but that reaction had such horrible consequences. I knew then that I needed to be punished. Everyone involved needed to be punished, but that was an unprecedented situation. Something like that had never happened before.

There was a guy in the front row that night calling me and Jermaine names during the entire game. He yelled at us constantly. That kind of thing I was used to. I could get yelled at by fans. I've been booed many times. But nobody in the stands had ever thrown anything in my face, so I was not prepared for that.

I certainly wasn't prepared for what was about to happen to me and the Pacers.

David Stern didn't waste any time. He announced that Stephen, Jermaine, Ben Wallace, and I were suspended indefinitely. He called the whole thing "shocking, repulsive, and inexcusable." He promised to start an investigation. Larry Bird was thinking I'd get 10 games. When he heard Stern was going to come down hard, he thought maybe I'd get 30 games.

The day after that, Stern provided the specifics. Stephen was suspended for 30 games and lost $1.7 million in salary. Jermaine was suspended 25 games and lost $4.1 million. Ben Wallace only got six games and lost $400,000. I received the largest suspension in league history—the remainder of the 2004–05 season and the playoffs. It ended up being 86 games and costing me almost $5 million in salary. That remains the longest non-drug suspension in NBA history. Nine players received suspensions with over $10 million in fines and 146 games total. David Stern wanted to make an example out of us and me in particular.

It felt like everybody in the world hated me. I lost all my endorsements. No more sneaker deals. All my commercials came off TV. All that shit was over. It was more shocking than scary, because it was all gone in the blink of an eye. The media continued to twist the situation. I would read headlines that made it look like I started the brawl. It felt like everyone from all of the networks were in cahoots and working against me. That got me mad. Even today whenever people talk about what became known as "The Malice at the Palace," they seem to only talk about me going up into the stands. They don't talk about Ben Wallace trying to fight me. They don't talk about the refs not controlling the situation and not ejecting Ben before the situation could escalate. They don't talk about John Green throwing a cup of Diet Coke at me. I reacted and I accept responsibility for my own actions, but I didn't initiate that situation. If the league couldn't control the fans from hitting me in the face with a cup of Diet Coke, what did they want me to do? Stand there and take it? There's no way I was gonna let a motherfucker do that. Get the fuck out of here. I wasn't raised that way. If I had not stood up for myself back in Queensbridge, I would've been eaten alive. If somebody hits you and you do nothing, they'll go and do it again. They'll keep bullying you. I wasn't even thinking. I was reacting.

The day after the brawl I was on *The Today Show* with Matt Lauer. The reason I went on TV was to promote my group, Allure. I was the manager and the label. They had a great R&B album. Great women. Great voices. The album was coming out November 23. I had a lot of money invested in that project, but my season had just ended, so I had no more money coming in. I felt like I had to do something to promote the album. Matt Lauer told me he was going to let me talk about it. He knew my situation, but as soon as I started to talk about the group he made it seem like I was out of control.

My relationship with the media began to change. Reporters had always come to me looking for stories and quotes because they knew that I'd say absolutely anything. I wasn't as mature back then so I didn't hold back. People took advantage of that after the brawl. I was friends with a lot of people in the media, but I found out there were those who would act like my friend one moment and then say bad things about me the next.

The brawl was serious enough to be taken to court. I was one of five players charged with assault and battery. Seven fans were charged as well, including Ben Wallace's brother. I plead no contest to misdemeanor assault. The two fans who walked onto the basketball court were charged with trespassing. The fan who threw the chair was charged with a felony. John Green was sentenced to 30 days in jail for throwing the cup that started the brawl. They revoked his season tickets and he was banned for life from the Palace. The players involved received one year of probation, 60 hours of community service, a $250 fine, and anger management counseling.

I wasn't the only person whose career was hurt by the brawl. Jermaine told me how hard it was for him to talk to his daughter about what happened. I guess she found out on her own. I know Stephen Jackson said the incident changed the way people saw him around the league. He was viewed as a thug. He wasn't. Not only was he a great champion, he was one of the best teammates I've ever played with, because he had my back. I hadn't even played with Stephen that long but he was the first one up in the stands with me. That's the type of loyalty you don't see that often. I completely understand where he was coming from, because I would have done the same thing for one of my teammates. If the roles were reversed and it was one of my guys up in the stands, I wouldn't have been able to live with myself if I didn't have his back. But still, he got into a lot of trouble because of what I did and that's hard to take.

I was suspended for the rest of the season, but I had to move on. I had to deal with it. Martin Luther King and Malcolm X went through a lot worse. A lot of people have been through a lot worse, so I'm not going to complain about some bullshit. That's why my math background came in handy because I had to figure that shit out.

That's not to say losing basketball wasn't difficult. I may not have let anybody see it, but it was so hard for me to be away from the game and my teammates. It almost made me feel like a different person. I walked around not wanting to talk to anybody, so I spent a lot of time with my kids. I'd drop them off at school and pick them up. Diamond was going to day care at the Indianapolis Jewish Community Center where I also worked out. I put in time on my album. I had some charities and scholarships that I was trying to put together. I tried to stay busy. The time off was good for my body, but I wish I could have been out there on the court. I was watching every Pacers game. Sometimes I'd go down to the arena after they played at home so I could talk to the guys.

A lot of people around the league reached out to me. Michael Jordan invited me to come down to his office, which was cool. Shaq was one of the guys who called me. He told me to hang in there. That kept me strong. Elton, Lamar, and those guys I had known for a long time reached out to me. Drew Gooden said some things on TV, so it was nice to hear that there were some players out there who had my back.

Larry Bird supported me and turned down numerous offers to trade me. A lot of people around the league couldn't understand why and thought the Pacers should cut ties with me immediately. Those people thought I was a liability. And I was at that time, but Larry acknowledged the mistake I made and was willing to move on. The team respected my game and respected my effort. I just wanted to win and Larry understood that. If I didn't have that passion, nobody would have put up with me. It's like what Artie Cox and Ray Polanco used to say—my intensity was my biggest strength and my biggest weakness. Never was that more clear than after the brawl. My aggression and intensity was what got me into that mess and resulted in basketball being taken away from me, but it was also what kept me in the league and would allow me the chance to get back what I had lost. I knew that if I let that incident change me too much, I wouldn't be the same player and I wouldn't be valuable to the team.

Another guy who took care of me at the time when I needed it was Pacers general manager Donnie Walsh. Donnie was like an uncle to me. He was always hands-on because he knew I needed that help. He was the one who really encouraged me to work on myself. It was bigger than basketball with Donnie. It felt like he was more worried about me as a person than he was about winning games.

/The court case went on for a long time and there was a lot of media coverage. The players union appealed the suspensions on behalf of Stephen, Jermaine, and me but Jermaine was the only one to get his suspension reduced. He missed 15 games instead of 25.

The Pacers went on to have a decent year without me. Those guys went through a lot. Jermaine and Stephen had to keep going to Detroit for hearings. I heard they had to get work permits just so they could go to Canada to play the Raptors. The fans in Indiana continued to come and support the team, but it was a disappointing year. The Pacers finished 44–38 and had the sixth seed going into the playoffs. They got bounced in the semis by the Pistons, who made it to the Finals and lost to the Spurs. That Pacers team was never the same and the organization wasn't in contention for an NBA title again until 2013. The guys who stayed on the team have spoken about the impact the brawl had on the organization. They said that it felt like a cloud hung over that team.

That year was also Reggie's final season in the NBA. I didn't know that at the start of the season. I don't even think the Pacers knew. Reggie was waiting for the second half of the season to announce his retirement. He had the chance to go out on top because we could have gotten him a ring that year. Winning that one game against the Pistons sent a statement. We had just beaten the defending NBA champs on their court. We dominated them. We proved that we were the team to beat in the NBA, but we ruined it. I tried so hard not to put all the blame on myself, but I feel like I ruined the final season of Reggie's great NBA career. He says that I didn't, but that's what Reggie is like. He's never going to blame me or say that I cost him a shot at a title, but it's hard for me not to feel like I did.

But I couldn't go back and change anything that happened. I could only move on and focus on the next year. My goal was still to win it all. I owed Indiana a championship. It was the least I could do for how well they all treated me during that whole mess.

It felt like I had been away from organized basketball for years when training camp rolled around in 2005. It was the first Pacers training camp without Reggie Miller since 1987. When we were down and needed somebody to take the game-winning shot, everybody in the building knew who was getting the ball. I only got to play with Reggie at the end of his career, but he was still clutch. I watched him do the impossible. Now he was gone. We had drafted Danny Granger in the off-season, and we still had Jermaine O'Neal and Stephen Jackson, but losing Reggie to retirement left a void. The organization was looking to Jermaine to step up, but we all needed to elevate our game.

I acted like everything was okay, but it clearly wasn't. I began the year with the best intentions but things went south quick. It started when I hurt my wrist. That happened in the fourth quarter against Cleveland when LeBron James fouled me. I had an X-ray and it wasn't broken, but I had to sit out until it could heal. I wasn't the only one with injury problems. Jermaine and Jamaal wound up getting hurt as well.

When I heard a rumor that the Pacers were considering trading me to the Sacramento Kings for Peja Stojakovic, I lashed out, telling a reporter for the *Indianapolis Star* that I didn't like playing for Rick Carlisle and that the team was holding me back. I wanted to be a scorer like Kobe and that if given the opportunity I could prove that I was a top-10 player in the league—not just a great defender. I didn't think I could do that in Rick's system because I wasn't getting enough shots. I wanted the ball because I felt like I had the advantage over whoever guarded me. Just because I liked to pass the ball and play defense didn't mean I couldn't score if given the chance.

I also wanted to be paid like a top-10 player. The Pacers gave Jermaine a $100 million contract and I was getting $40 million. I didn't feel like I was being compensated the way I should have, and I let that get to me. I was an All-Star and a Defensive Player of the Year. Apparently you didn't get max money for defense and hustle. You needed to score. Given my reasonable contract, I knew the Pacers would get trade offers for me. I really wanted to go to the Knicks, and even back then I was talking about maybe going to Cleveland so I could play with LeBron, but there was more to it than me wanting the ball and more money.

I never let on how much pressure I felt after the brawl. To be honest, I did not want to go back to Detroit in a Pacers uniform. I was scared of what might happen and I didn't want to do anything stupid in the heat of the moment. Asking for a trade may have been premature on my part, but I just wanted to take a step back and reevaluate my career. I was still mentally unstable after the brawl. Even if the Pacers gave me max money, I don't think things would have worked out for me in Indiana. I felt like I couldn't escape my past there. I had too much baggage. A part of me wanted to retire and walk away from everything.

Larry and Donnie heard about me asking for a trade through the media. I didn't come to them directly, so they fined me $10,000. Donnie decided that he didn't want me practicing with the team anymore. He thought I was a distraction and he was right. They were tired of it and I don't blame them. They had no idea what I might do next. In early December of 2005 I was placed on the inactive list while the front office tried to work out a trade. My agent reached back out to the Pacers after the holidays to see if they were willing to let me stay, but that was off the table.

Some of the guys on the team took it personally when I said I wanted to be traded. They felt like they had stood by my side during the suspension, only for me to walk out on them. I also didn't come to them first to talk about it. They were right to feel that way. That's why I've always wanted to go back in time to Indiana and play with Jermaine, Stephen, Jamaal, and Jeff Foster so we could accomplish what we set out to achieve. Indiana was the place where I wanted to finish my career. It got messy and I was unprofessional. I wish I had handled that situation differently.

SACRAMENTO AND HOUSTON

Chapter 15

Sactown

Meanwhile, I waited.

It took over a month for a deal to be worked out. A lot of teams were mentioned. The Kings, Clippers, Lakers, Atlanta Hawks, Golden State Warriors, Minnesota Timberwolves, and Denver Nuggets all came up. There were rumors of three-team deals. After a while it felt like I could end up anywhere. I heard that I was going to the Clippers in exchange for Corey Maggette, but that trade fell through after Corey hurt his foot.

While I waited, all I heard about in the media was how much of a problem I was and how I would be a distraction in any locker room. I had my issues and I screwed things up for myself in Indiana, but what was being said about me in the press wasn't entirely true—at least that's not how I viewed myself. I had another side and the people close to me knew that I was also a caring person who gave back as much as I could. A lot of the people who were speaking out against me at that time, or saying I was a liability, didn't know me personally. I tried not to let that get to me but it was hard to do so.

There had been talks between the Pacers and Kings for a while. Peja was about to be a free agent and it made sense for the Kings to get something in return rather than letting him walk. When it looked like the trade would fall through again, the Pacers called me into the office. They explained that my agent was hesitant to endorse the deal because he felt Sacramento had limited endorsement potential for me. I tried not to think about that. After all, it was difficult to tell what my endorsement potential even was after the brawl. But those things were no longer an issue for me. I just wanted to play basketball and at that point I was happy to go to Sacramento or any other place that wanted me.

I had one brief conversation on the phone with Kings owners Joe and Gavin Maloof. I told them that I wanted to be there. That was all they needed to hear. On January 24, 2006, I became a member of the Sacramento Kings.

The Maloofs owned the Palms hotel and casino in Las Vegas, and they gambled on me by giving me a chance. I respected that and I was excited to be a King. It was a breath of fresh air to be in a new city and playing for a different team. I knew my past would never be totally forgotten, but in California I felt a step removed from the brawl. I wasn't under the same type of pressure.

Rick Adelman had been the head coach of the Kings since 1998 and he took them to the playoffs every single year. A few years earlier the Kings had been one of the best teams in the NBA and led the league in wins. Sometimes called "The Greatest Show on Court," that team had Mike Bibby, Chris Webber, Doug Christie, Vlade Divac, and Peja. They could have won a title but they missed their window. Webber hurt his knee and in 2005 was traded to the 76ers. Christie and Divac were also gone. The Kings were trying to rebuild their roster and had gotten off to a slow start in 2006. They were 18–24 at the time of the trade.

I joined the team in Boston. It was also Wally Szczerbiak's first game with Boston, after being traded from Minnesota. Peja had been playing well for the Kings. He was averaging 16 points per game before the trade, so they needed somebody to step in and contribute right away. It was difficult to fill Peja's shoes because the fans loved him and he had been playing with Rick since he started coaching the Kings. I felt that I needed to make my presence known and scored seven of the team's first 15 points against the Celtics. I got off to a good start but we lost that game.

It is always difficult to join a new team in the middle of the season. It was even harder being thrown into the starting lineup with a bunch of guys I had never played with before and expected to contribute, but that's part of being a pro basketball player. It was a sink-or-swim situation. Luckily, I had been in that situation before with the Pacers, so it wasn't new to me. Once I got to Sacramento, fitting in on the court never became an issue.

The difficult part was life off the court. I moved my family down from Indiana and we had to find a place to stay. It took some time for my wife and kids to adjust. We lived in a hotel for a while, which made things difficult. I was living out of a suitcase, but I soon found a house and settled in. I kept my place in Zionsville, Indiana, and my family and I would frequently go back there. My kids ended up staying in school in Indiana. To me, Indiana always felt the most like home. That's where I signed my first big contract. It's where I got married. That's the place I started to see all my hard work begin to pay off. Even today, Indiana is special to me.

I did my best to stay focused on basketball because that's why the Kings acquired me. I told everyone on the team that we were going to the playoffs. They thought I was crazy, but Rick Adelman said to me, "Ron, the team will go as far as you can take us."

Bibby was the go-to guy. It was his team but every play was coming through me, so I had a chance to make an impact. I had a great year in Sacramento. I averaged 16.9 points that season and made first-team All-Defense.

Rick Adelman became a basketball father figure to me. That season, he really taught me what it meant to be a good teammate. That's what I needed after all I had been through in Indiana. I was caught up in my own hype and the pressure of being a scorer and an MVP candidate, but playing for Rick helped me put that in perspective.

After I joined the Kings, we went 26–14 and beat out the Jazz by three games to be the eighth seed in the West. That meant a matchup with the top-seeded Spurs. We were thinking upset, and given the way we were playing, it wasn't that far-fetched. But we lost Game 1 bad, 122–88. During the third quarter, I was called for giving Manu Ginobili an elbow to the face and had to sit out Game 2. That was my reputation coming back to haunt me, because that wasn't a foul that I should have been suspended for. If you go back and look at the video, you can see that I didn't hit Ginobili with an elbow. What I did was no worse than the elbow that Manu hit me with at the beginning of the game. That happened on the very first possession. I went out to guard Ginobili and he lost the ball. While we were scrambling he caught me with an elbow that busted my lip. It stunned me and I went down. He got called for a foul, but he got to stay in the game. When I committed a similar foul, I had to sit out the next game. That's just the way it was going to go. I accepted the suspension. I had to deal with it and figure out how to keep playing my game.

Kevin Martin took my place for Game 2 and played unbelievably well. The whole team played tough and took the Spurs to overtime, but we lost 128–119. We were coming back to Sacramento for Game 3 and I was back in the lineup. Something was in the air and we could all feel it. That game came right down to the wire. With 30 seconds left, the Spurs were up one with the ball. I guarded Ginobili as he took the ball up court. I locked him up. I wouldn't let him go by me. They tried to set a screen for him, but Bibby played great help defense. He knocked the ball loose and it went right to Kevin Martin, who drove down the court and scored over Tim Duncan to beat the Spurs by one right at the buzzer.

In Game 4, Bonzi Wells was on fire and led us to a 102–84 win. The series was tied 2–2. Bonzi showed up again in Game 5, scoring 38 points, but we just didn't have enough. The Spurs won that game and took Game 6 easily to win the series, but it was the closest 4–2 series I had ever been in. If a couple things went differently we could have taken down the Spurs. That was our series to win. I had been telling everyone we had a shot from the minute I got there, but after seeing how close we came, I think the rest of the team started to believe that we could do something special.

I saw how well Bonzi Wells was playing and told Rick that we should start running some plays through him. I wasn't wrong. He averaged 23 points and 12 rebounds in the playoffs. That was probably the first time I thought that I might make a good coach someday.

I was focused on winning in Sacramento and not worried about personal stats. I had proven that I could lock people up and I knew that I could score, but I would sacrifice being in the limelight to win a ring. I couldn't have said that the previous year in Indiana. That guy who complained to the media about not getting enough shots, that was never me. It was not how I grew up playing the game. I was much more comfortable sharing the ball and playing team basketball. Sacramento was where I did a lot of maturing on and off the court.

One of the guys I have to thank for helping me is Corliss Williamson. I had such great respect for Corliss. He was the ultimate professional and a true vet. At that point in my career I wasn't as reckless as I had been a few years earlier. I was finally able to listen to what people were saying to me. Corliss was one of the first guys to get through to me. He really taught me a lot on and off the court. He was a guy who never gave up and helped to push that team into the playoffs.

It may have looked like I was back to my old self again, but I wasn't playing with the same confidence. I didn't realize it at the time—and wouldn't realize it for many years—but I was still scarred from the Malice at the Palace. My game never fully recovered and I never got back to that level I was at in Indiana, when everything was clicking. I had put on weight, but the bigger problem was that I wasn't able to heal mentally after the suspension. I told myself and everyone else that I was back but I was not the same player.

I still had that will to win. That never changed, and I could feel it begin to catch on with the rest of the Kings. We had been playing so well down the stretch that I didn't want the front office to break us up, so I offered to donate my salary and play for free if the team kept Bonzi Wells and Rick Adelman. That didn't happen. Both Bonzi and Rick left for Houston. Right after the series with San Antonio, the team announced it wasn't renewing Rick's contract. There was some talk of Don Nelson being hired, but it was former Golden

State head coach and recent Memphis Grizzlies assistant Eric Musselman who became the new head coach.

I played with the team in the Las Vegas summer league. That league is mainly for the younger guys or the new players on the team, but I didn't care. I just wanted to go out and play against some good competition. I didn't know much about Eric Musselman, but he was coming in with a group of brand-new assistants, so there was a completely different system we had to learn. It felt like we were starting from scratch.

Unfortunately, that next season didn't pan out very well. Eric Musselman was a great guy. He was a family man and a really good person, but he was not the best fit for that team.

It's easy to say it now, but I think we would've had a much better season if we kept Rick Adelman. He had the most wins in franchise history. I guess the owners and the GM hadn't been happy with Rick and wanted something more from him, but I don't think getting rid of Rick was the answer. It all went downhill from there. The Kings haven't been back to the playoffs since that loss to San Antonio, and since Adelman left, they have gone through nine different head coaches.

The Maloofs did things their own way. They were different than some of the other owners. While I played in Sacramento, they were good to me. They called me the "face of the franchise," and it was great playing for owners who believed in me and wanted me there. One summer the Maloofs came back with me to Queensbridge. They walked around the projects without any security. You don't see many billionaires hanging out in the projects, so I had to respect them for that.

The Maloofs even offered to play some of my songs in the arena during games that season. My first album, *My World*, was released on Halloween in 2006, and that could have been some good exposure for my own music career, but I had to turn them down—at least until we were playing better.

That first album of mine was a long time coming. Nature helped me write my first rhyme back in 1997. I started writing my own rhymes and rapping in 1999 because there were things I was going through that I wanted to write about. I grew up listening to some of the R&B classics my parents played in the house, but as I got older my taste evolved. I got into rap and hip-hop. I wanted to talk about my experiences and what I saw growing up. The problem was it was difficult to put my best effort into music because the league was so demanding. I had a limited amount of time. I had done some touring with Allure back in the summer of 2004, but that burned me out. I hadn't yet learned how to balance music with basketball. No matter how much interest I had in music, basketball always came first. I had to pass on a lot of opportunities in the music industry because I couldn't let basketball take a back seat.

I wasn't making music to make millions of dollars. I wanted to prove myself and show people that I could make good music. I had a couple different artists signed to my Tru Warier label and we went on a 30-city tour over the summer to build a fan base. We opened for Young Jeezy and Ludacris. We went to Europe with Fat Joe. I liked being on stage and performing in front of a crowd. I still do it to this day and I hope that I can keep on doing it. Hearing a good song is like an adrenaline rush. I like being able to get the crowd at a show riled up. Watching people sing along with my lyrics is a different type of experience that you can't get on the basketball court.

If I could go back to that time, I'd do a lot of things differently when it came to putting out that album. I felt like I was holding back lyrically. I might have been a little too worried about how I came off and tried too hard not to step on any toes—especially since David Stern had squashed Allen Iverson's rap album. David did that because of the controversial things A.I. was saying on his album. I wasn't saying anything controversial, but it was still in the back of my head. An even bigger mistake was not letting anybody help me. I didn't use any outside producers or engineers. I was so competitive that I wanted to do it all on my own, but I didn't realize that I needed a talented team around me. Basically, I needed a coach. I was learning as I went along. I didn't have any melodies and that's what adds color and life to the lyrics. My album got a lot of bad reviews, but I had a passion so I kept pushing and I got better. That's the story of my life.

Chapter 16

Breaking the Cycle

The day my life changed forever was March 5, 2007. That was the day I got into an altercation with Kimsha at the house. She called the police. As they were leading me away in handcuffs, I saw my daughter watching. That was one of the worst feelings I have ever experienced.

The Kings suspended me indefinitely, but that was not what was on my mind or what worried me the most. There was no excuse for what happened and there is no way to describe how bad I felt about that entire incident. That was a much different feeling than the way I felt after the brawl.

Five days after I was arrested, I made a public apology to my wife and my family. I apologized to the Kings, my teammates, and to the league. I was in tears. The Kings allowed me to return to the team. The league said it would review the case and might still hand down a suspension. In the meantime, I was allowed to play.

I felt incredibly lucky to get another chance. It was a second chance that brought me to Sacramento to begin with, so I was running out of chances, but this wasn't all about basketball. It was so much bigger. I wanted to make things right with my family. Getting back on the court was the easy part.

Kimsha dropped the charges but I was still indicted. On May 3, I was sentenced to 20 days in jail. I was able to serve 10 days in a work-release program and had to complete 100 hours of community service. I also had to pay $600 and was placed on three years' probation. The court insisted that I attend parental counseling and anger management counseling. The NBA even found me a marriage counselor. Sometimes I was doing three sessions a day.

It was time for me to make a choice. *Do I stay this angry person and walk through life thinking that everyone hates me, or do I try to improve?* I was tired of myself and I wanted some answers. What happened to the kid who loved Michael Jackson and wanted to be a math teacher or an architect? *Where did I go wrong? I wasn't always like this.*

I had seen a lot of therapists over the years but I didn't always listen and I didn't always take their advice. Whatever I had been doing wasn't working, so I decided to rededicate myself to becoming a better and healthier person. It was hard, but not only did I get used to those sessions, they turned my life around. Counseling allowed me to take a critical look at my life and see where I had gone wrong.

I had my own anger issues. That's been well documented. What I learned in counseling was that I was dealing with real issues when I did that stupid shit out on the court. It wasn't just me being crazy. Together, my therapist and I examined the root of those issues. I learned what triggered my destructive behaviors, how to avoid those triggers, and what to do when I felt myself losing control. When I was finally able to really heal, and not just put a bandage on some of those problems, it felt like I was unstoppable. That was a great feeling.

Our marriage counselor was the absolute best. He and I went back to when I was four years old and opened up every single wound I'd tried to forget, and some I didn't even know I had. I was so young when some of those things happened. He asked me to talk to my mom and dad about my childhood, and I found out things I had no memory of. He then had Kimsha and I tell the truth to each other about all the things we had done. That was crazy, but we did that. We had been through a lot and talking about all of it was painful at times, but it helped us get to the root of our problems. It helped us to better understand each other and where we were each coming from. Because of that counseling, Kimsha and I learned how to talk to each other about anything.

On top of that, I attended parental counseling. For a long time I hadn't been raising my kids the right way. I was fucking up. I may have been providing for them financially, but that wasn't enough. As a parent, you have to be there for your children in every way they need, and for a long time I wasn't always there. All of my therapists and psychologists helped me so much and I feel that I'm a much better father today because of it. I have a great relationship with all of my kids. Most importantly, I learned how to deal with myself when facing all different types of situations. I better understood what the real problem was.

When I would fight with Kimsha in front of our children, I was repeating exactly what I saw my parents do as a kid. Kimsha grew up the same way. It was normal for kids growing up in the hood to see their parents fight and for the police to arrive. It was easy to get used to that and assume that was the way things were supposed to be. My mom and dad were always there for me as individuals, but not as a unit. I saw the lack of love my father showed my mother. I never once saw my father come home with a rose for my mother. When parents don't show that love toward one another, they're sending a message to that child whether they intend to or not. I never saw the correct way to raise a child. You can be a good person but you learn how to be a parent by growing up in your own household. As a result, I started doing the same things my parents did. Kimsha and I would argue. I was messing around. My parents never said "I love you" to me when I left the house, so I never said "I love you" to my kids when they left the house. I was repeating a pattern. My relationship with my wife and kids was dysfunctional and I didn't understand why. I felt bad about it and I tried to suppress those feelings with alcohol and marijuana. I thought that would make everything okay for a little while, but it just made everything so much worse.

That wasn't a problem unique to my family—it's a cultural problem. Look at the black families who grew up in the ghetto. How did that behavior originate? Where did we get it from? Our ancestors came here from other continents. They became slaves and were separated from their children. So who was raising those children? A slave master didn't care. Fast-forward a couple hundred years and there are children out in the streets right now who are going through the same things those children went through. We don't always have strong morals or values because we don't have strong family units passing those values down from one generation to the next. Now kids are raising themselves, or worse, being raised in the street. That only contributes to the violence and the drug use and the poverty. It creates a community of some crazy motherfuckers who will do whatever they have to do to survive—even killing their own people if they have to.

How can we reverse that? Those of us who have become successful and have gotten out have to go back and give back. We have to tell our stories so these kids know that anything is possible. We have to treat our partners well. Being a good partner is one of the most important things in life. That's often overlooked. I overlooked it for so many years, and I often wonder how different my life would be if I had been a better partner who was there for my kids and kept our family together.

I didn't want to be the type of father who got hauled off by the police in front of his daughter. I didn't want to be a father who wasn't there for his kids. I had to learn from my parents' mistakes in order to break the cycle. Kimsha and I had to learn how to leave what we saw growing up in the past. We had the chance to make things better for our kids so they wouldn't have to endure the things we did. If we do our jobs, then our kids can make it even better for their kids, and so on.

I started to engage more with my kids. I asked them about their day and I spent as much time as I could with them. Doing that can't help but bring you closer. When it comes to family love, I know what it is and what it shouldn't be. When I was able to give and feel that genuine family love, those were some of the best times of my life.

When my court-mandated sessions were over, I wanted more. I learned so many different things from all my counselors. They changed my life. I better understood who I was and why I made so many mistakes during my life. I was beginning to have more control over myself and my emotions. After seeing how much all of those classes helped me, I became passionate about counseling and improving myself.

After the brawl and my arrest, I felt compelled to do twice as much as I'd been doing when it came to charity and helping different communities. Life was bigger than sports. People looked up to me and I wanted to make sure that they saw me doing something right and not just getting into trouble. When I'd return to Queensbridge, I often wondered if my behavior had any influence on the kids I saw. I didn't want that to happen.

Back on the night I was drafted, all of the players who were there in the building got together in a room with David Stern. I asked him, "What are you doing for the urban communities? I know you have the NBA Cares program, but what are you doing inside those communities?" All of the other players looked at me sideways. They thought I was crazy for saying that to Mr. Stern. I was only 19, but I really wanted to know what the NBA was doing to help.

There are a lot of black people who become successful and never give back. They change. I never wanted to be one of those people. When I was in Indiana, I gave back to a poor white community that had a high school dropout rate. It wasn't just black kids or poor people who needed help, but I felt like I had to give back to my people first. I came from the ghetto so I had an obligation to help those who grew up in a similar situation. The ghetto needed someone in its corner.

So many people thought that I was being negative when I talked about the ghetto or told people that I was hood. I wasn't promoting that lifestyle. I wasn't a thug or a gangster. To me, it was just the reality. You had kids going to jail for drugs and guns. They didn't realize that those guns and drugs being brought into the community would only hurt their own people. We were killing our own people just to make a little bit of money on the side. Some felt like it was the only choice they had. Too many black kids think that they can't change. It's my job to tell black kids that if you make a mistake, get back up on your feet. There are too many neighborhoods

Named after my father, Ronald Artest Sr., I grew up in the Queensbridge Housing Projects in Long Island City, New York.

When it came time to pick a college, I liked the idea of staying in New York and chose to play at St. John's. (AP Images)

Getting drafted by the Chicago Bulls in 1999 was a dream come true. It also meant I got to play with my old AAU teammate, Elton Brand. (Newscom)

It was an honor to play against Michael Jordan when he was with the Washington Wizards. That's why I felt so bad about breaking his ribs during a summer pickup game. (AP Images)

The Bulls traded me to Indiana in 2002, where I joined a talented roster that included the great Reggie Miller. I thought we were on track to win an NBA championship...

...Until the Malice at the Palace changed the course of NBA history and almost derailed my career. I carried the baggage from that night with me for a long time. (Top/Bottom: AP Images)

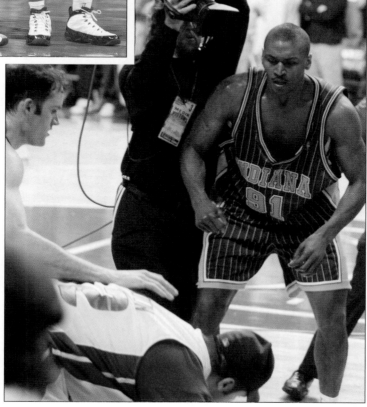

The Pacers eventually traded me to Sacramento. I hadn't lost my desire to compete, but the scars from the Malice at the Palace still had not healed. (AP Images)

In 2008, the Kings traded me to Houston, where I thought we had the makings of a contender. Unfortunately, injuries to Dikembe Mutombo (middle), Yao Ming (right), and Tracy McGrady kept us from reaching our goal. (AP Images)

After years of rumors about me moving to Los Angeles, I finally became a Laker in 2009, joining Kobe Bryant (middle) and my old friend from New York, Lamar Odom (right). (AP Images)

I was so excited after we beat the Boston Celtics in the 2009–10 NBA Finals, it took a while for the reality of the situation to sink in. I was finally an NBA champion. (AP Images)

By the time the Lakers let me go in 2013, I had officially changed my name to Metta World Peace. I was happy to join Carmelo Anthony as a member of my hometown New York Knicks, but things didn't work out and I was bought out after playing only 29 games. (USA Today Sports Images)

People didn't think I was serious about going to play overseas, but I signed with a team in the Chinese Basketball League for the 2014–15 season. I got a lot of press after I talked about changing my name to "The Panda's Friend." (AP Images)

As I got older, giving back to the community and raising awareness about mental health issues became more important to me. I raffled off my Lakers championship ring to raise money for charities (top), visited the A Place Called Home youth center in South Central Los Angeles (middle), and traveled to Washington, D.C., to support the Mental Health in Schools Act (bottom). (Bottom: AP Images)

I was happy to return to the Lakers for the 2015 and 2016 seasons, and during my last home game in Los Angeles, the fans showed me their appreciation. (AP Images)

It wasn't a 60-point performance like Kobe Bryant's last game, but I started and scored 18 points in the second half, much to the delight of my young Laker teammates. (AP Images)

where kids aren't worried about education because survival is more important. I want those people growing up in poverty and surrounded by violence to realize that there is another path. You don't have to sell drugs. You need to stay in school. You need to get an education so you can get a job you enjoy and live a healthy lifestyle, one that doesn't negatively impact yourself or your neighborhood. I wanted to help those kids who were still stuck in the hood and let them know they could elevate themselves. We all make mistakes but you have to learn from them.

The season was over by the time the league decided on my punishment, so they suspended me for the first seven games of the following season. I didn't hear the news right away and couldn't be reached for comment because I was in Africa. I had joined fellow NBA players Theo Ratliff, Etan Thomas, and Maurice Evans on a charity mission to Kenya. It was organized by Kermit Washington, who worked with the NBA and the nonprofit Feed the Children organization. The idea was to deliver 11 million pounds of rice to the needy families living there. Seeing the conditions in the slums of Kenya was unreal. Some areas had no water or electricity. Babies were infected with HIV. Children were running around without shoes or clothes. You might see that kind of stuff on TV, but it's much different when you're there in person. There were wild animals within an arm's reach. Hippos were in the lake. Bats would fly into the tent where we slept at night.

I didn't always like to talk about that stuff. Not because it wasn't a worthwhile cause, but because it was often viewed as a PR stunt to repair my image. Some people were always going to take it that way, but if me mentioning it and talking about those issues could raise awareness and get those people the help they needed, then it was worth it. People in America don't realize how good we have it and how difficult life can be in those third-world countries. Some places have no running water. There are no toilets. I grew up in the hood, but at least I lived in a building and had access to food. That's not that bad compared to what I saw in Kenya. That trip to Africa really opened my eyes and motivated me to do more when I came home.

I began putting together my own foundation, called Xcel University. The idea was to provide educational scholarships and opportunities for kids growing up in unfortunate situations. I also wanted to use the organization to promote mental health awareness. There were probably a lot of kids who struggled with the same things I did. I knew I wasn't the only one. Some kids might have felt like they were different and didn't know why. I wanted those kids to know that someone understood what they were going through and that they were not alone. I was fortunate that I had the money to afford those services, but kids on the streets couldn't pay $100 an hour for therapy. If I could provide services to those kids, or introduce them to professionals, it could help them reach their full potential. So many people had helped me growing up. It was my turn to do the same thing for someone else.

I wanted something good to come out of something negative. If getting arrested and suspended led to me becoming a better father and a better person, while giving me the opportunity to change other kids' lives, then it wouldn't be a waste. Something similar happened to Hank Carter, the businessman who took me into his home my senior year of high school. He grew up on the streets, but after witnessing his friend be paralyzed by a gunshot wound, he turned his life around. He went on to start the Wheelchair Charities, his foundation that provided wheelchairs and services for patients in New York City. Just like Hank did, I wanted to find a similar way to turn a negative into a positive.

I felt that I was improving as a person. I felt more stable. I felt that I was a better husband and father. Unfortunately, things on the court were starting to fall apart. Even though I was just coming off one of the best seasons of my career from a statistical standpoint, the Kings weren't winning. Eric Musselman had been fired after one year and the team brought in Reggie Theus as the new coach for the 2007–08 season. I had to serve my seven-game suspension. Kevin Martin got hurt at the start of the season. Mike Bibby was traded to Atlanta in the middle of the season. We finished with a losing record and didn't make the playoffs for the second straight year.

I had one year left on my contract and I had a chance to opt out, but that wasn't even on my mind. Sacramento was where I wanted to be. I really embraced that city. I had started appearing on a local radio show with Carmichael Dave on KHTK. It wasn't every night; I could pop in when I wanted to. That was fun because I could go to the studio once the kids were in bed and just bullshit. We'd take some calls and talk to fans. Sometimes I'd tell stories. I also did some commentating for the Sacramento Monarchs, the local WNBA team. I wanted to find a way to get into the media world, but that didn't happen right away. TNT and ESPN weren't interested, but I was able to conduct a one-on-one interview with Kobe Bryant for *The Best Damn Sports Show Period*. It was really cool to sit down with Kobe, who was still one of my idols even though he was only a year older than me.

I saw Kobe again later that year. It was in Boston after Game 6 of the NBA Finals, where the Lakers were blown out 131–92. I just went to the game as a fan. I wasn't invited by anybody. I even wore my Kings shirt because at that time I was still hoping to re-sign with the Kings. I'm not the type to jump ship and I didn't want anybody thinking I showed up there because I wanted to be a Laker.

After the game, I walked into the locker room. I went back into the showers where Kobe was by himself. He was pissed off after the loss. I tapped him on the shoulder and scared the shit out of him. He had no idea what to think. I know from experience that when your season ends the way it just had for the Lakers, all you can do is think about how to get back and be better the next year. So I told him, "Don't worry, you're gonna get them next time." That was really it. People made it out to be more than it was.

I was under the impression that the Kings would sign me to an extension before the start of the next season. When that didn't happen, I no longer felt that same love from the Maloofs. There was miscommunication between me, my agent, and the front office. I had the chance to opt out of my contract and become an unrestricted free agent, but I didn't take it and immediately wished that I had. It was a mess and I was mad at myself because it felt like I made a bad business decision, so I let it be known that I wanted to be traded.

I still wanted the chance to play for my hometown Knicks, but there was also talk that I would be traded to the Lakers. I always preferred to try to beat the best than to play with the best, but that situation was different. Lamar was my best friend, I was a fan of Kobe's, and I grew up idolizing Phil Jackson when he was the coach of the Bulls. I always thought Phil was the type of coach who could get something special out of me. If the opportunity presented itself, I would absolutely go to L.A., but when that fell through, it was back to waiting again. This time, I was going to be my own agent. I didn't want there to be any miscommunication. I wanted to know exactly what teams felt about me so I could go to a franchise that wanted me.

Chapter 17

In Houston,
We Had a Problem

Houston was not on my radar as a possible destination, but at the end of July I learned that I was going to the Rockets as part of a five-player trade. Nobody saw that coming. Everybody thought I was going to the Lakers—even me.

Being a Rocket meant that I would be playing for coach Rick Adelman again. We got along great in Sacramento and he was one of those coaches who could get a lot out of me. It always seemed like the game came easy to Rick. He was like the Michael Jordan of coaches. He won games wherever he went. Hell, he won 22 in a row for the Rockets the previous year. It didn't matter what organization he was coaching—if you gave Rick Adelman good players, he would get the most out of those players and win games. Bottom line.

Houston had the players. Tracy McGrady had led the league in scoring twice and was on his way to becoming a Hall of Famer. Tracy and I had some wars over the years. We had respect for each other and I knew he was hungry for a ring because of how hard he competed. The problem was that he had been battling injuries for the past couple of seasons. The Rockets also lost Steve Francis, who had joined the team the previous year but never fully recovered from a quad injury. But the injury that hurt them the most was when Yao Ming went down with a stress fracture the previous February and missed the rest of the season.

I was excited to play with Yao because he was one of the few guys in the league who was completely unstoppable when he was healthy and on his game. He was strong and fundamentally sound. Combine that with the fact that he was so damn big and there was only so much you could do when trying to guard him. I felt that he was going to get his ring sooner or later.

In the beginning I thought Yao and I might get off on the wrong foot. When he heard about the trade, he expressed some concern to reporters. He said something about having to win now if it was going to work and hoping that I wouldn't run up into the stands again. I wasn't sure how to take that, but it did catch me off guard. I talked to my dad and he said not to worry. So when the media asked me for my response to Yao's comments, I didn't want to make waves. I just told them that he probably never played with anybody who represented their culture the way I do.

As soon as I met Yao we were cool. I understood where he was coming from and I knew that he didn't mean what he'd said maliciously. In fact, I can say that Yao Ming was probably the best teammate I ever had. He was a superstar in the NBA and he was even bigger in China, but he was so incredibly humble. He was a down-to-earth guy. He never traveled with security. He had a ton of money but he didn't flash it around. He drove a little beat-up truck. Yao was a team guy. He never put himself above the rest of us. He always did everything the team did and he practiced hard. He was a great player and a great leader.

The previous season everyone watched the Celtics win a title with the trio of Paul Pierce, Kevin Garnett, and Ray Allen. Why couldn't Yao, T-Mac, and Artest do the same thing with the Rockets? But it wasn't just Yao and Tracy who made the Rockets great. The whole team was deep and we had some great veterans. Brent Barry was a guy with two rings. I looked forward to playing with Shane Battier. He was such a great defender, so I knew we could complement each other by sharing defensive assignments. Yao was 7'6" but backing him up was Dikembe Mutombo, who was a four-time Defensive Player of the Year. He was at the end of his career but still stepped up big when Yao went down the previous year. I knew Mutombo. He had given me some good advice over the years. Also on the Rockets was my old teammate from the Rucker League, Rafer Alston. It was pretty cool to be able to catch up with him in training camp.

I had one year on my contract and I wasn't thinking beyond that. It was all about the Houston Rockets and what we could do right away. I was content to be the third or even the fourth option if need be. Whatever Coach Adelman asked me to do, I was going to do, and at the beginning of the season that meant coming off the bench to back up Shane. I thought I deserved to start but if that was how Coach Adelman felt I could best serve the team, that's what I was going to do. I had proved that I could score, in Indiana and Sacramento. I was more confident and comfortable in my offensive game, and I didn't need to put up big numbers to feed my ego. It was Yao and Tracy's team. They didn't need me to go in there and be the man. I wasn't going to disrupt the chemistry they had already developed. My job was to adapt and adjust to my new team.

One thing I did want to do was give that team a spark. I wanted to get them thinking not just about the playoffs, but about a title. The Rockets hadn't gotten out of the first round of the playoffs in 12 years. It almost felt like a curse, because they had the talent. If Yao had been healthy the previous year, they could have competed for the title. If that was the case, I probably wouldn't have been on the team. They already had the pieces, but now with everyone back and healthy, we were going to give teams problems. I told the media that people were going to stop saying "Houston, we have a problem," because Houston was going to give other teams problems.

I knew an opportunity when I saw one, and at that point in my career I wanted to take full advantage of it. We had the talent. We had the experience. We had the drive. If we put it all together we had a chance to win the championship. We just had to stay healthy.

The city of Houston welcomed me with open arms. All the fans came out for a big rally they held for me at the Toyota Center. It was like a sea of red when I walked out there onto the mini-stage they had set up for a press conference. It was really cool. I hadn't experienced anything quite like that before. Seeing that made me even more excited to play for the organization and those fans.

I may have been living in Houston, but I still needed to finish some of my court-appointed therapy sessions, so I started shopping for another mental health doctor. That's when I found Dr. Santhi Periasamy. She's the psychologist who I would later thank after the NBA Finals in 2010, but I started seeing her back in 2008. She worked with a lot of different patients and spent a lot of time with athletes, so she could definitely understand my situation.

Dr. Santhi helped me keep a low profile. I'd go to her office at night when there weren't many people left in the building and she always went out of her way to help me. I spilled my guts to her during those sessions. I knew I was ghetto and I didn't care what people thought. Combine that with my quick temper and it was a destructive combination. As soon as anyone challenged me or disrespected me, I lost control. Dr. Santhi helped me calm down. We worked on focus. I would text her before games when I got nervous. She would always take the time to reach out. She'd walk me through various breathing exercises and I would relax. It almost felt like I was free in a way that I hadn't been before. Sometimes we just talked about basketball.

I didn't meet with Dr. Santhi just to get my mind right. I also met with her so I could become a more effective player on the court. When I brought my baggage with me onto the court, I'd become confrontational. Then I'd get fined and suspended. She helped me learn how to control that, because I couldn't become a better player and help my team if I wasn't on the court. Controlling my anger made me feel like a better person. We also talked about the pressure I felt and how it could bleed over into the other areas of my life.

I didn't solve all of these problems in Houston. I don't think anybody ever "solves" everything. It's about managing your problems and trying to improve your situation. Breaking down and dealing with each problem individually sounded simple, but it was hard to do when it seemed like so many different things were going wrong in all different areas of my life. Just focusing on the pressure related to basketball helped me deal with that problem. It was all a state of mind. And once you improved that one issue, it naturally improved other issues and made dealing with problems more manageable. Pretty soon I noticed a change in my game. Things got better for me mentally. I wasn't as anxious or nervous. I let the game come to me and that was such a more comfortable way to play.

If I had found Dr. Santhi earlier in my career, I wouldn't have had nearly as many problems on the court. The brawl would still have been the brawl—that wouldn't have changed. I'm talking more about the techs, the flagrant fouls, the suspensions, and the fines. When I got hit with that cup in Detroit, I was reacting. I know better now, but back then I felt that I had something to prove. It wasn't always about basketball. Sometimes it was about who was tougher on the court. I wanted to bring the street to the NBA. It took me years to learn that the NBA wasn't the same as the street. There were no guns or drugs on the court. I was the one who had to learn how to change. Reacting the way I did was a waste of energy. In the end, it didn't mean anything. It didn't prove anything and it sure as hell didn't help me win any games.

It was Dr. Santhi who encouraged me to reach out to John Green, the guy who hit me with the cup in Detroit. Not only was I facing my fears and directly talking about the incident that had changed the course of my career, I also thought it would be a good way to show the kids how two people could come together and put the past behind them. I went on Twitter and asked if anybody could help me find John's phone number. Somebody from Chicago found it so I called his house. His wife answered.

"Hello, this is Ron Artest. Can I speak to John please?" I said.

She was surprised. It sounded like she thought somebody was messing with her, but she gave the phone to her husband.

"Hello, Ron."

He said it like he was expecting me to call.

Each of our lives had been turned upside down by what happened, but enough time had passed that we were able to talk about the incident without getting upset. He even apologized.

"It was stupid. I shouldn't have done what I did. I'm sorry," he said.

He meant it. We had a good conversation that day and we're still cool today. I don't hold any grudges.

Because of Dr. Santhi, the Rockets got a Ron Artest who was more in control of his emotions, but no matter how much I tried to avoid unnecessary confrontation, trouble had a way of finding me. On October 30, I received my first technical foul as a Rocket, but it happened while trying to break up a fight during a game against the Mavericks. Yao had been fouled by Josh Howard. I saw them starting to get into it so I ran over to break it up, because I didn't want Yao doing anything that would get him thrown out.

In spite of all the talent in Houston, we could never get going as a team like we wanted to. We never played up to our potential, and then in February it looked like the whole thing was going to fall apart when we lost Tracy McGrady for the season. The Houston Rockets could not escape injuries. Injuries destroyed that team the previous year and they were destroying the team again.

Tracy had back problems and knee injuries throughout his career, but somehow he was still one of the league's best scorers. He had knee surgery before the season and thought he was healthy, but he never got back to full strength. He missed 18 games and then in February opted for microfracture surgery, which put him out for the rest of the year. Tracy would never recover from that surgery. He just couldn't stay healthy. He soon turned 30 and bounced around to a couple teams before going to China to play. He eventually came back to play his final season with the Spurs. It's a shame, because Tracy McGrady was such a special player. He's one of those guys who always comes up in that discussion of what they could have been had they not been hurt. In terms of natural talent, he was up there with Kobe and LeBron. I really would have loved the chance to be out there with him when he was 100 percent.

Some argue that we were actually a better team without Tracy McGrady. We did have a better record: 20–15 with him and 37–16 without him. We were scoring more points and shooting a better percentage from the field, but to say that we were a better team without Tracy wasn't entirely true. I did call Tracy out for not playing good enough on defense at times, but he was a superstar and you couldn't replace that. We may have improved as a team, but if we had a healthy Tracy McGrady, I think we would have improved even more. Tracy wasn't the problem.

We finished 53–29, but we lost the last game of the season to Dallas and fell to the fifth seed in the West. That was not where we pictured ourselves at the beginning of the year but we were in the playoffs, which meant we had a shot. Personally, I had a decent year even though my role was limited and I split time with Shane Battier. I still averaged 17.1 points with 5.2 rebounds and 3.3 assists, but none of that meant anything if we couldn't get past Portland in the first round.

Yao and Tracy may have gotten all the attention, but what really made that team click were veterans such as Brent Barry. He had won two NBA titles with the Spurs. He had been there before. The rest of us hadn't. Even though he wasn't putting up big numbers late in his career, he was a leader. He'd always tell us to never take our foot off the gas. If we were up 10, he didn't want to see us coast. He'd push us to go up 20. That's what separated the good teams from the great teams—the ability to put the other team away when you had a big lead and to not let them back into the game.

That's exactly what we did to win Game 1, but we were up against a good young Portland team. They had LaMarcus Aldridge, who was starting to emerge as a big talent, but the guy on that team who was a killer was Brandon Roy. He could get hot at any time and lead his team back. In Game 2 he dropped 42 on us and we lost by four. I knew Brandon Roy was good, but I didn't know he was that good. His defense wasn't quite there yet, but that performance in Game 2 left an impression on me. I told Craig Sager that he was the best player I'd ever guarded. All the guys in the TNT studio gave me a lot of flak for that comment. In that same interview I also said Charles Barkley was overrated, so I guess I had it coming. I admit that I might have gotten carried away when saying Brandon was the best player I ever guarded, because that title goes to Jordon, LeBron, or Kobe, but Brandon Roy was one hell of a player. It's a shame that his career ended early due to injuries, because he could have done some serious damage in the league if he had stayed healthy.

We were up 3–2 on the Blazers going into Game 6. We had just let them off the hook in Game 5 so we came out aggressively. Von Wafer came up big for us and he wasn't even on an NBA roster at the start of the year. Aaron Brooks started to show us what he could do. He filled in for Rafer Alston, who was traded earlier in the year. Even though we had the lead at the end of the game, it was important that we finished strong. Everybody was hustling. Yao was driving for loose balls. I ran up into the stands going after a loose ball. We didn't let up at all. Getting used to playing like that was so important. Like anything else, it's all about creating good habits.

Our team continued to play hard, but the fans started celebrating before the game was even over. God bless Houston, because those fans were passionate. They loved our team. I wanted to play for fans like that, but at the end of the game I grabbed the mic and asked them to give Portland a hand. I didn't want to see our fans get out of line or disrespect the Blazers, because that was a team that played hard. The fans gave them a round of applause so it all ended well.

I'm glad the fans finally got to see us get past the first round, but I had bigger goals. We were facing the Lakers in the next round and we needed to stay focused, because we knew the Lakers weren't celebrating any first-round win. For franchises like the Lakers and the Celtics, the season was a failure if they didn't win a title. If you wanted to compete on their level, you needed to have that same mindset.

The Lakers had an entire week to get ready for us. They were the top seed in the West. They had the best record in the league and they were also the highest-scoring team in the league. Nobody gave us a chance, but in a sick kind of way I always liked situations like that. I loved to prove people wrong and do the impossible.

At the end of the regular season, I promised Von Wafer that I'd cut my hair into a mohawk like his if we got out of the first round. I did not want to be walking around with a mohawk, but I'm a man of my word so that's what I did. However, I added a little twist. When I was first traded to Houston, I had the Rockets logo shaved into my head. I had done something similar when I was with the Kings. The fans and the media loved it, so when I got my mohawk, I had the Rockets logo shaved into the side. Why not?

I did not have a good series against Portland. I was taking a lot of bad shots. I missed a lot of threes and wasn't consistently scoring like I had during the regular season, but on that Rockets team I didn't need to score. Even without Tracy in the lineup we had a team full of scorers. We didn't have guys putting up huge numbers, but we had a roster of guys who could be counted on to step up and contribute. If Aaron Brooks was having an off night, Kyle Lowry would step up. When Luis Scola got into foul trouble, we could turn to Carl Landry. That worked on the other side of the ball as well. When we played the Lakers, Shane would guard Kobe a lot, but then sometimes I'd switch over and guard him. We tried to mix it up and throw different looks at him—anything that might throw him off of his game. One time that worked during the season and we got Kobe frustrated, but there was another time when it backfired and Kobe went off.

The series against the Lakers was physical from the opening tip. In Game 1, Shane took a shot to the head and had to get a couple stitches. He had blood running down his face. For the rest of the series fans held up giant posters of a bloody Shane. That's the image I remember when I think back on that series. It represented our mindset. We went out there looking to beat down the Lakers. We wanted to be the tougher team. We got off to a great start because we did what nobody thought we could ever do—we took Game 1 on their home court 100–92.

If Game 1 was physical, Game 2 was a war. Scola and the Lakers' Derek Fisher went at it. Scola was coming over to set a pick and Fisher just curled up and checked him. Fisher was ejected for that. Things got heated on both sides in the second half. Kobe, Scola, Luke Walton, and Lamar Odom all got hit with techs.

Kobe and I had been battling all game. Every game against Kobe was a battle, but during Game 2 he kept slapping my hand away when I tried to guard him. I was allowed to reach out and touch him. I was playing very basic defense, but Kobe kept slapping my hand away. I told the refs but they didn't say anything, so Kobe kept doing it. "Keep playing like that," I told Kobe. "Keep slapping me. Keep hitting me. I'm not going to react."

We kept going at it. In the fourth quarter we were battling for a rebound underneath the basket when Kobe caught me with an elbow to the neck. I ran down the court and got right in his face. The whistle blew. Players and refs rushed to break us up, but I wasn't going to do anything physical. I just wanted to look him in the eye, confront him, and let him know that he had to cut that shit out. I would never back down to anyone—I didn't care if it was Kobe Bryant. I could take his elbows, but win or lose I wanted the game to be fair. I thought the refs let that game get a little too out of hand. I was expecting to get a tech, but Joey Crawford ejected me. Still, I kept my cool. I didn't agree with the decision, but I accepted it. That was my past coming back to haunt me again. There was nothing that I could do so I had to let it go.

We were down 2–1 in the series when we learned that Yao had broken his foot in the previous game. As if the Houston Rockets hadn't been through enough the past couple years, Yao Ming was out for the rest of the playoffs. Dikembe tried to fill in for Yao like he did the previous year, but then we lost him to an injury. We were running out of big men, but the thing I always loved about that team was our toughness. We didn't quit. We used that as motivation and came out to win two out of three and force a Game 7. Everyone stepped up their game. Aaron Brooks, Luis Scola, and Carl Landry all picked up the slack. I even got Kobe frustrated enough during Game 6 that he lashed out and got called for a tech.

We were the tougher team for most of the series, but by Game 7 we had finally run out of gas. Our lack of size and all of the injuries caught up with us. The Lakers had a good squad. They overcame some adversity that year and went on to beat the Orlando Magic in the NBA Finals to win it all, but I'm proud of what our Rockets team did that year. Even though we were 0–4 against the Lakers during the regular season, we took them out to deep water and pushed them to the brink in a seven-game series. Had Yao not gotten hurt, that could have been a very different series. And who knows what kind of damage a healthy Tracy McGrady could have done in the playoffs? But injuries were part of the game. We weren't the first team to catch a bad break.

Meanwhile, my contract was up. I enjoyed my time in Houston, but everything changed for the Rockets with Yao and T-Mac hurt again. The team decided not to sign me to a long-term deal. At first I was mad at Houston, because they only offered me a one-year contract when they had a chance to use the Larry Bird exception to exceed the salary cap and sign me to an extended deal. I thought they should have treated me better, so once again I was left to explore other options.

LOS ANGELES

Chapter 18

I Love L.A.!

If it had been up to me, I would've gone back to play in Indiana after my time in Houston had ended. I would have gone there for less money because I felt that I owed them a few good seasons. A part of me also really wanted to go play in Greece. I had visited there years earlier and I always wanted to play in Europe. I also asked my agent if there was any chance that I could go to the Pistons. Detroit was a rough city and I was hoping that I could do some good in the community. Playing in that building every night would have been difficult given my history, but that's what I liked about it. I wanted to do things that were hard and make it look easy. I would have loved that opportunity, but the Pistons weren't able to make a deal at that time.

Then I got a call from my agent telling me that the Lakers were interested. There had been rumors about me going to Los Angeles for years but the timing was never quite right. Everyone thought the Lakers would re-sign Trevor Ariza, so I never even considered them as a possibility. But they didn't re-sign Trevor and that opened up cap space for me. The time was finally right and the stars aligned. Ariza ended up signing with the Rockets to replace me, so we basically swapped teams.

I met with Lakers owner Jerry Buss in Los Angeles and had a call with Phil Jackson. Phil spoke to Kimsha, which I thought was pretty cool of him. Even Magic Johnson gave me a call. The whole organization made me feel wanted. Playing for a team that wanted me was just as important as being able to compete for a title.

I signed a five-year deal worth $33 million. That was a pay cut from what I'd been making, but I was fine with that if it meant that I could play in L.A. I was playing to win at that point in my career and having the chance to do that as a Laker was a dream come true.

Kobe reached out to me a couple times. Things got heated between us in the playoffs, but that didn't mean anything. We were both competitors and competitors go at each other. We were not friends when we played against each other on the court, but now the Black Mamba and I were on the same team. We were both wearing that golden armor and I was excited to see what kind of damage we could do together.

I showed up at their facility in early July to meet everyone and sign my paperwork. They had a camera crew following me around that whole day—and that was before the actual press conference. That's when I knew I had finally arrived in Hollywood.

At that press conference I announced that I was going to wear number 37. There's a story behind all of the jersey numbers I've worn. My dad's number when he played in high school was 51, so I flipped that and wore number 15 at the end of high school through my time with the Pacers. In 2002,

I switched over to 23 in honor of Jordan. A few years later I wore 91 because of Rodman. I loved how he forced the league to pay attention to defense. I wanted to represent my hood in Sacramento, and that's where 93 came from—it looked similar to the QB for Queensbridge. It was the same idea behind 96 in Houston but the lowercase version, with 6 being a lowercase b. I wanted a new number for my new start in Los Angeles. Somebody suggested I should be 42 because it was the opposite of Kobe, but 42 was James Worthy's number and it had been retired by the team. I decided on 37 because Michael Jackson's *Thriller* was No. 1 on the Billboard charts for 37 straight weeks. I loved Michael Jackson as a kid and I thought that was a way I could pay homage to him.

I was in a whole new situation in Los Angeles. I had joined a team that just won an NBA title a few weeks earlier. The Lakers organization had won 15 titles and wanted number 16. Phil had 10 and wanted 11. Kobe had four and wanted five. Derek Fisher had been with Kobe for all of those titles. Nobody in that organization was going to take their foot off the gas just because they won the previous year. Those guys were all hungry for another championship. The entire city was hungry. The only real difference between the Lakers I was joining and the previous year's championship team was me.

I hadn't won anything yet. I already felt that pressure, but I made it so much worse by telling the media that if we didn't win a championship in 2009–10, it would be my fault. That was stupid of me to say, and I was constantly reminded about that comment throughout the year. I basically invited the media to point the finger at me.

Not that I needed the motivation, but that got me to work. I was a bit overweight at 270 and managed to get down to 250. Playing hard during every practice and game will get you into shape. I also quit drinking for the most part, which always helps, especially when you get older. Something I really got into during that period was spinning. I had always thought it was just a bunch of girls in a room riding bikes, but I did that for 10 minutes and I was ready to quit. Spin class made me work because I didn't want to look like a fool in front of all those girls who weren't even breaking a sweat. Spinning was one of the hardest things I had ever done.

I knew I had to get ready to play with Kobe. I had known him for years, but I didn't know what to expect once I was on his team. I first played against him in high school and was in awe of him even then. The reason I loved playing against Kobe was because he challenged me and never backed down. I liked playing against guys who played hard. Not only did he play hard, but he never broke. It didn't matter if I stopped him three or four times down the court. He never got discouraged or changed the way he played. He kept coming back and never shied away from being physical.

Kobe practiced the same exact way he played. He would get to the gym at 5:30 AM in the summer and play all the way until 8:30. He'd be done and leaving right when everybody else on the team was just getting there. That's dedication and that's the guy I wanted to lead me. Not every franchise player was like that, and I've had some confrontations with other franchise players because they didn't lead by example.

I could relate to Kobe's passion because I was used to being the hardest-working player on the team. I wasn't a guy who went out to dinner with his teammates or talked to them about sitcoms. I was all about the game, and that's how Kobe was. When we were in the gym, we were trying to get better and trying to get an edge on our opponents. That was something we had in common, and after spending so many years in the league I knew that type of competitiveness and intensity was rare. That was the main reason I wanted to come to Los Angeles.

When camp started it almost felt like I had to prove to Kobe that I was worthy of being his teammate. You had to work to earn his trust on the court, and if you couldn't help Kobe win games, you couldn't help him at all. He was talkative. He was opinionated. He was always teaching. He demanded that everyone gave 100 percent. He pushed his teammates like no player I had ever played with before. Kobe would find your weak spot and apply pressure to see if you broke. Not everybody could handle that. He didn't coddle anybody and if you couldn't keep up you were left behind. That intensity was what set him apart. When he was in the room, you could feel the fire coming off him.

Practices were intense. Kobe was very stubborn but so was I. He'd talk and try to get under my skin. I would go right back at him. Pretty soon, we were throwing elbows at each other like it was a playoff game, but it was only practice. It was that kind of intensity that got us ready for games.

Kobe was like another coach, but not just during the game or even during practice. Kobe would coach us up on the plane. On one of my first road trips with the team, I was playing cards with some of the guys when Kobe walked up and tapped me on the shoulder. He motioned for me to follow him back to his seat. I put down the cards and joined him in the back, where he was already watching the tape of the game we had just played. He would run through play after play to point things out: "Look at this. Here is what you need to do in this situation." It wasn't just the big things. It was the little details. He paid attention to everything.

I went back to my seat and then watched Kobe go up to Shannon Brown and do the same thing with him. He did it with everyone. It didn't matter if you were sleeping—he'd wake your ass up. Kobe wasn't waiting for practice to get everyone on the same page.

I loved to pick Kobe's brain. I used to always ask him how he hit so many game-winning shots. He'd joke around and say something cocky, but he'd never really answer me. It took me a while to realize that the reason Kobe was successful was because he was so completely focused on the game. He never let anything take him out of his game or deter him from winning. Back when I was in Houston and got into that scuffle with Kobe during the playoffs, I got up in his face, but I was the one who was ejected. Kobe didn't pay any attention to me. He let it go and he stayed in the game while my ass was in the locker room. Good or bad, nothing could take his mind off the game. It wasn't about trying to hold it down or proving that you were the bigger man. Sometimes walking away was harder to do than fighting. Once I learned that I became a much more effective and reliable player.

I felt like everything I'd been through had prepared me for this opportunity with the Lakers. I was ready to win.

My first season with the Lakers got off to a great start. Pau Gasol sat out the first 11 games with a hamstring injury, but that didn't set us back. Lamar stepped into the starting role and then went back to being the sixth man when Pau returned. We were running teams out of the gym. The bench stepped up. It felt like we were unstoppable.

The team was playing well but I had trouble transitioning. Saying that I'd be happy taking a back seat was easier said than done. I was coming off a big year in Houston. Before that I averaged more than 20 points in Sacramento. I got to the Lakers and my average dropped to 10 or 11 points a game. Kobe was going to do his thing. Then there was Pau and Andrew Bynum and Lamar. I had never played with so many guys who could score the ball. At times it felt like I was literally the last option. I wanted to take over at times, but I had to learn what it really meant to be a role player. That was hard to do when you were used to being the man. Not getting those touches was frustrating, but what made things so much more difficult for me was that I felt like I was better offensively than I had ever been before. I think I could have averaged 25 if given the chance, but that was not why the Lakers had signed me.

The system in L.A. also took some getting used to. Rick Carlisle had a very specific way of running his offense back in Indiana, and Phil did things his way with the triangle. We ran a version of the triangle back in Chicago, but Phil's was different. It took me a long time to get comfortable on that end of the court because it had so many different levels and layers. It was about reading and responding, not set plays. It required a completely different mindset. I felt stuck. I had to learn how to let things flow.

That adjustment period created tension between me and Phil. Our styles clashed at the beginning of the year. It felt like he was singling me out. Phil was one of the few people who could really get under my skin. I think he liked to push people's buttons. But he also gave me some leeway when it came to my reactions. Not many coaches were like that. We got into it a few times and had some shouting matches. Finally, Phil took me into his office. He sat me down, closed the door, and said, "Enough is enough." I didn't understand exactly what he was doing until years later, but he was teaching me the right way to play. It was hard for me to grasp but I had to learn.

Phil was into Buddhism and he introduced me to the whole Zen thing. Every couple of weeks the entire team would meditate. He'd turn off the lights, burn some sage, and get us all to zone out so we'd be collectively thinking the same way. That's what got me into meditation. I learned how to identify those moments when I was tense or angry and transfer that negative energy into positive energy. I was able to apply that to my life and it's something I still do to this day. I love my singing bowl.

In the end, what Phil really taught me was patience. He used to tell me, "Patience is a virtue." It took me a while to realize what he was talking about, but I put it together. I made peace with my own situation. I let go of the fact that I wasn't the man anymore. I had the chance to be the man on my own team before, in Chicago and in Indiana, but I messed that up. I could easily be out of the league, but I was still here and still playing. It made me appreciate what I had. Once I learned to let go, my time came.

There was one game in 2010 when Kobe sat out against the Spurs. I finally had a chance to prove that I could still score, so I did my thing and dropped 18. That was enough for me, because there were more important things we needed to do.

We battled a lot of injuries that year. Bynum struggled with knee problems. We needed him in the lineup because he was a big guy who was a good finisher on offense and could alter shots on defense. Kobe broke the index finger on his shooting hand, but he pushed through. There were no excuses with Kobe and he didn't let any injury keep him out for long. If Kobe was going through pain, he wasn't going to complain about it. Kobe would play through a gunshot wound.

I wasn't spared from injuries that year either. After playing against LeBron and Cleveland on Christmas Day, Phil allowed us to go home and spend the night with our families before we flew out to Sacramento the next day. Since my daughter would open any gifts that were left out in plain sight, I had hidden them outside. I grabbed them all and started walking up the porch to the front of the house. I remember falling, but that's it. I was out. My wife woke me up. She was crying.

I had no idea what was going on. I didn't know where I was. I got to the hospital and they told me that I had a concussion. I also needed stitches to close a cut on my elbow. I ended up sitting out for five games.

At the end of the year we pulled it together and got the top seed in the West, but that didn't mean anything if we didn't play hard. That year we definitely did not have an easy first-round opponent. Oklahoma City was not the typical No. 8 seed. That Thunder team wasn't a title contender yet, but they were getting there. It was their first trip to the playoffs, but we didn't look at them as being inexperienced. Everyone in the league knew their potential. They had the youngest roster in the league and still won 50 games that year. Scott Brooks had just won Coach of the Year. Kevin Durant was the scoring champ. Russell Westbrook was in his second year, but he had some great games and started to make a name for himself. They also had James Harden, who was making an impact as a rookie.

Before the start of the series, I decided to dye my hair blond. I had always done different things with my hair and that year was no different. On opening day, I had the Chinese word for "Champion" cut into my hair on one side and "Chatty," the name of a friend of mine who had passed away, cut into the other side. Later in the season I wanted to do something different, so I went on Twitter and asked the fans for ideas. I decided to have the word "Defense" in Japanese, Hebrew, and Hindi shaved in. That didn't work out so well for me, because Vince Carter dropped 25 on us the day I did that. I shaved my head soon after. When it was time for the playoffs, I got talked into dying my hair again, by D.J. Mbenga.

I guarded Durant during our playoff series, but this time I wasn't treating it like it was me versus Durant—it was the Lakers versus the Thunder. We were a unit, but I still needed to do my part and Durant was a tough cover for me. The top scorer in the league was always going to be hard to stop. He was going to get his touches and score some points, but I was going to make sure he had to take a lot of shots to get his numbers. It was my job to deny him the ball when I could and force him to take bad shots. Kevin was long. He's a 6'11" shooting guard so nobody can block his shot, but I guarded Durant just like I guarded everyone else in the league.

A lot of guys watched tape and studied other players before matching up on defense. That worked for some people, but it wasn't something I ever did. I didn't want another player taking me out of my game or forcing me to do something different. I wanted to do the opposite. I was going to play my game and force the other player to make adjustments. That's not to say that I never made adjustments, but I went into the game looking to play everyone the same.

It worked. We got off to a good start. Durant struggled and it helped us jump out to a 2–0 lead in the series. The Thunder came right back and won two games on their home court. Durant hit some shots in my face, but I stayed focused. We closed out the series by winning the next two games. That was a tough series and you could tell that the Thunder were going to be good. They had three future superstars and solid role players who would make their mark on the league in years to come.

In the next round, we swept the Jazz and advanced to play against Steve Nash, A'mare Stoudemire, and the Phoenix Suns in the Western Conference Finals. That series was similar to the OKC series. We won the first two games, but the Suns won the next two to tie it at 2–2.

Game 5 was epic. In a way, it kind of summed up my first season with the Lakers. We had an 18-point lead in the second half but the Suns clawed their way back. With about a minute left we were up three. I got the ball near the top of the key and missed a jumper, but Pau got the rebound and kicked it back out to me on the wing. I immediately went up for a three and missed again. Phil was mad. The whole arena was mad. That wasn't the right play. With that much time on the shot clock, you're supposed to bring the ball out and set back up.

I was just trying to stay aggressive. I was trying to put the team up six. That's what I was thinking at the time. I was trying to make things happen for the team, but I forced it. Sometimes that year I tried to go for the home run when it was not the best play to make. Phil was very upfront when telling me what he thought about my three-point shooting. That got in my head. It had me hesitating at times when I touched the ball. Phil would encourage me to attack and use my body when going to the basket, instead of settling for threes and jumpers. That's what I should have been doing.

Phil was upset but he kept me in the game. On Phoenix's next trip down the court, Jason Richardson banked in a three to tie the game with three seconds left. We had one last chance to win in regulation. Lamar inbounded the ball to Kobe, who took a wild three. I was on the opposite wing. From my angle I thought he got fouled. I assumed the shot would be short, so I went after it. It seemed like everything was moving in slow motion. Everyone else was standing around watching Kobe's shot because it felt like a buzzer-beater. I nudged out Jason Richardson and was right there under the basket to catch the ball when it fell short. I went right back up and made the layup to give us the win. I didn't react at first. I was going to run off the court, but then I saw the fans go crazy. Everyone was so excited that I got caught up in the moment and jumped into Kobe's arms.

Craig Sager talked to me after the game. That was the interview where I got him to say "Queensbridge." That was my most memorable moment with Craig, who was always such a great guy and brought so much to the league. It was a sad day when he passed away, and I definitely miss Craig Sager.

That game-winner got me out of a slump. The media kept asking me questions and wanted to talk about the good things and the bad things that happened during that game, but I wanted to forget it. We still hadn't won the series yet. We hadn't accomplished anything. I had to put it out of my mind and move forward, but that was hard to do because everyone kept reminding me about it. It didn't feel like I won Game 5. It felt like we had to go right back out there and win Game 6.

Immediately after that game I went to the local sports club to work out. That year I used to go to a bunch of different sports clubs around the city. Working out the night after a game was a way to keep your body fresh; it also gave you more time to recover, since you could take the next day off and have fresh legs on game day. When I was younger I used to work out two, three, and sometimes four times a day. That was stupid. You shouldn't work out four times a day. As I got older, I learned not to work out as much and saved that energy for the games. Some of my best games and shooting performances came on days after I rested my body. That was exactly what happened in the Phoenix series. I picked it up in Game 6 and had my best performance so far that postseason, but Kobe's 37 (nine in the last two minutes) helped give us the series win. We were moving on.

The 2010 NBA Finals. Lakers versus Celtics. It was the 12th time that the Lakers faced the Celtics in the Finals, and it was a rematch of the 2008 series, which Boston won. I wasn't on the team for that loss, but there wasn't much talk about revenge or wanting to get another shot at the Celtics.

We approached it like a fresh series and the Celtics were a different team. Rajon Rondo had come into his own and basically turned the big three of Pierce, Allen, and Garnett into the big four.

Everyone on the Lakers had been to the Finals before but me. It was my first time playing in June, but ever since my rookie year I always made sure to work out until July, so my body would be ready for that situation when it arrived. Ever since I was a kid my goal was always to win the championship. I achieved that goal at La Salle but hadn't experienced that feeling for 13 years. That was a long time and there had been a lot of seasons that ended in disappointment since then. Now I had my chance to win again on the biggest stage there was. I also knew how blessed and lucky I was to be there at all. I told myself that no matter what happened, I was going to thank God for the opportunity.

I had to guard Paul Pierce again. I played against Pierce twice in the playoffs back with Indiana. He was older now but he was still moving well. He could still attack. He hit big shots in big games and had already won a title. Boston would certainly put his jersey up in the rafters one day. I respected his game. If I didn't, I was going to be in trouble. And after all those years, Paul Pierce was still the best trash talker in the game. He was probably the last big superstar who could talk trash because none of the stars today can talk. It's a dying art.

On the first series of the first game I got tangled up with Pierce and we both hit the floor. I wasn't trying to get into a tussle. We were both playing hard and that's what happened. It was championship basketball. There wasn't a message being sent. We both knew what the stakes were. I had always been a physical player, so I didn't have to go out of my way to do that stuff anymore. I was still an aggressive defender, but I was more calculating at that point in my career. I kept my composure. It was more about strategy. I focused on moving my feet to cut him off and forcing him to take bad shots.

We took Game 1 but the Celtics came back fighting in Game 2. That one was all about Ray Allen. My mind was on stopping Pierce, but Ray hit seven threes in the first half and broke the NBA Finals record when he hit his eighth three in the second half. Rondo had a triple-double and the Celtics went on a 16–4 run to win the game and tie the series.

The next three games were all in Boston. We split Games 3 and 4 to make the series 2–2 going into Game 5. Bynum was playing hurt. Kobe kept us close, but Garnett and Pierce were too tough. Late turnovers killed us. Thankfully, the last two games were in L.A. A lot of people counted us out, but that's why we didn't pay any attention to the media. We destroyed the Celtics in Game 6 to set up the first Game 7 in the NBA Finals since 2005.

I was having a good series defensively. I was able to keep Pierce in check and he wasn't going to the foul line, which was where he did a lot of his damage. Offensively, I struggled. I missed a lot of shots. I didn't trust myself. I wasn't always playing with confidence. I was nervous and getting caught up in the moment. My teammates were pulling for me. They believed in me the whole year, but I kept hearing about how the team might have been better with Trevor Ariza. It was Trevor this and Trevor that. I brought all of that on myself. I told the media that I didn't care about scoring, but when reporters would talk about how I only scored two points, I'd get in my own head and then tried to go out there to score more. There was a lot of pressure and I didn't perform well when under that type of pressure.

The person I turned to for help was Dr. Santhi. Even though my court-mandated sessions were over, we'd still talk every couple of weeks. At the beginning of the season she helped me adapt into my supporting role on the Lakers. She helped me become a better teammate when I found myself feeling selfish. I reached out to her again during the Utah series and that's when we started talking regularly.

I told her the pressure was getting to me. The mental part of the game was always difficult for me. I was starting to get caught up in my own head, instead of going out there and playing. She flew out to Phoenix and then she flew out to Boston. I was a nervous wreck, but she was able to help me relax. She told me to think about my team and trust myself. We'd do my breathing exercises together. She told me to breathe the same exact way when I was out on the court. She taught me to keep an even keel. I didn't get too high or too low. That was what I focused on and it helped me block everything out.

I had to get back to basics. I had to keep it simple. All I had to do was go out there and play. Shoot if I was open and try not to think about it. Phil was helpful. He was there reminding me to stay focused. He told me not to worry and not to get down on myself. That was all I needed to hear. It meant a lot coming from Phil and it made me more comfortable.

Game 7 did not get off to a good start. We lost any momentum we had from Game 6 as the Celtics took an early lead. In the second half they were up 13, but we battled back. Derek Fisher was the one who pulled us all together before the fourth quarter.

"Relax. Don't look at the score. Just go out there and play," he said.

He was like a guardian for that team. People always tried to count him out, but he was in great shape and paid attention to detail. He was getting older but he was still effective because he was smart and rarely made mistakes. When Fish talked, we listened, and slowly we clawed our way back. With six minutes left, it was Derek Fisher who tied the game with a three. We took the lead and were up three with one minute left. I was 60 seconds away from a championship.

Kobe had the ball on the wing. I was standing outside the three-point line when Kobe got in trouble and passed me the ball. He immediately looked for me to pass it back to him, but I saw my opening. I had the shot. I didn't think about all the threes that I had missed in the past. I didn't think about the criticism I received back in Phoenix for shooting too quickly. I wasn't thinking that it was the final minute of Game 7 of the NBA Finals. I had blocked all of that stuff out, so at that moment it was just another shot. The trick is realizing that the shot you take in the playoffs is the same shot you take back in the park. It's no different. All that changes is the stage. It's the media and the fans who make it into a big shot, but at that time all I saw was a shot that I was confident I could make. I jab-stepped at Paul, who stepped back a little bit. That gave me some space, so I took the three and it went in.

The game wasn't over yet. Ray Allen and Rondo kept the Celtics in it, but we held them off to win the game. After the buzzer sounded, it still hadn't sunk in that I was an NBA champion. I was ready to keep playing. It didn't seem real. I looked over at Kobe and he said, "We won!" Only then did I realize what had just happened.

I had played that moment out in my head so many times before. I told myself that I was going to keep it all about the win by walking off the court. I wasn't going to speak to the media or anything. I just wanted to enjoy the moment with my family. Well, that all went out the window. I got caught up in everything that was happening around me. I was just so happy.

People today talk about what happened after the game just as much as they talk about what happened during the game.

By the time Doris Burke interviewed me on camera, I was an emotional wreck—but in a good way, for once. To have Game 7 of the NBA Finals end the way it did was unbelievable. I had always dreamed of hitting a shot like that in a Game 7, and now I had done it. I couldn't put that feeling into words. We were in front of our home crowd. Confetti was coming down from the rafters. I don't even know what Doris said to me. I started thanking my family and everyone who showed me support throughout my career. I definitely couldn't leave out Dr. Santhi, because she really helped me so much during those final days of the season. It wouldn't be right to leave her out, and I wanted to give credit where credit was due.

I guess the idea of admitting to seeing a therapist was taboo for a player in the NBA at that time. Some people thought it was weird, but I was never afraid to improve myself or share my experience. I felt that it could help others the same way that it helped me. I meant it when I said that I couldn't have done it without her. It felt like I was stuck on a boat in the middle of a storm and she was the one who led me into calmer waters. She's the reason why I had a clear head when Kobe passed me the ball near the end of Game 7.

Once it sunk in that we were champions, I started thinking about alcohol. I had never had champagne that tasted so good. By the time I got to that press conference, the champagne had definitely kicked in. My family joined me and it was great to have them all there. I saw my dad standing behind me and thought of all the times we used to play full-court one-on-one at 4:00 in the morning back on 12th Street. My mom, my wife, my kids, and my brother were all there. It was too much. I've watched that press conference a bunch of times since then and I still have no idea what I was doing. The whole thing just seems so wild and out of control, but it was beautiful. I was so happy to be there, but it was also important that I took the time to acknowledge my old Pacers teammates. We had a chance to win it all when I was there. I felt like a coward for leaving Indiana the way I did. I carried that around with me for a very long time and I never had a chance to really talk to any of them about it. That's why I apologized.

I had thought about winning an NBA championship since I started playing basketball. When it finally happened, it really was everything that I thought it would be. I felt that I had it in my blood. I finally had a ring, and to know that I played an important role in earning it was an absolute blessing. When I was younger, I sometimes questioned myself and wondered if I was wasting my time by working so hard. That moment suddenly made all the hard work worthwhile. I knew my career would continue to have ups and downs, but no matter what happened, nobody would ever be able to take that accomplishment away. I still remember that feeling to this day.

Chapter 19

Bigger Than Basketball

I put so much pressure on myself during the playoffs and I was so in the moment that I wasn't able to enjoy the ride. But now the ride was over. We won. It was my time.

Right after the press conference, we started at the steak house across the street from the Staples Center and then went club hopping. I wore my game jersey, sneakers, and warm-up pants. We were all over town. After the club we stopped by Dr. Dre's Interscope Studios to see Polow da Don. There was more champagne. We played some ping-pong. Everybody in there was smoking marijuana—except for me. I gave Chris Brown the game jersey off my back.

Dr. Dre happened to be there that night and I played my song "Champions" for him. The single was coming out in a couple of days, but I had recorded the song when I first got to L.A., before the start of the season. I had played it for the guys in the locker room and wanted the song to become an anthem for the team. It wasn't just about the Lakers or even basketball. It was a song for anyone who wanted to be a champion, and that included parents and role models. It was crazy to see how some of the lyrics in that song played out in real life during Game 7.

Dre listened to the song and said, "I think we can record this better."

Dre put me behind the mic and started coaching me up. He broke down each syllable in every word. By the time we got to the second verse, it was 5:00 in the morning. I was drunk and probably high as hell off all that secondhand smoke. My eyes were closing. I couldn't keep going.

Dre told me, "Come back and we'll finish the record."

This can't be real. Dr. Dre offered to help me with my single. That was a dream come true. Opportunities in the music world don't get much bigger than that—but I didn't take that opportunity. My dumb ass never called him back. Can you believe that? I never called Dr. Dre back! I was too intimidated. That remix of "Champions" is probably still sitting in his studio.

The next night the whole team went on *Jimmy Kimmel Live!* and then there was the parade, which was crazy. I decided to wear a top hat my daughter made in art class. It had pink feathers but I couldn't say no to her. The day after that I went on *The George Lopez Show* and got to perform "Champions." I loved the music and I loved performing that song, especially since we won. I played that song nonstop. My kids got so sick of it and begged me to play something else in the car, but that wasn't happening. The song later got included on the NBA 2K11 soundtrack.

It felt like that championship vibe lasted the entire summer. Lakers fans were everywhere and the city was so happy. Los Angeles was a city with lots of stars, so I would get congratulations from people such as Oscar De La Hoya and Alyssa Milano. She and I met when I was doing a telethon at CNN for the disaster in the Gulf with Larry King. It was crazy to meet someone I grew up watching on TV. Things like that made experiencing the title in Los Angeles seem unreal at times.

The Los Angeles Lakers were champions, but it wasn't long before I started thinking about winning the next one. I definitely savored and appreciated this one, because I knew how easily that Game 7 could have gone the other way, but winning was like a drug. Even though we had just won, I couldn't wait to go back and do it all over again. I was ready to get into the gym immediately.

It was back to business for a whole new season. The championship was in the past. We had big goals for the next season, but nothing was going to change. We had to practice the same way we always practiced and play the game like it was supposed to be played. As always, Kobe set the tone by showing up ready to work.

All the talk that year was of the Miami Heat. They had just signed LeBron and Chris Bosh to play with Dwyane Wade. The Heat were suddenly the preseason favorites and people kept asking us about the Heat, but we didn't pay any attention to them. We focused on our team. It's not like I needed any motivation. Nothing motivated me more than I already motivated myself. I felt like I was still getting better as a player. I was comfortable in the triangle. I was starting to get into the flow. I was in my prime. When the fans and the media doubted me, I stuck with it. When people told me not to shoot, I played my game. Hitting those shots in the playoffs and winning a championship took a lot of the weight off my shoulders.

I fought with Phil a lot during that first season with the Lakers, but in the end he was right. He took all of the different egos and personalities on that team and he made it work. He got us to put everything that didn't have to do with winning off to the side. That's an area where a lot of coaches fail, but he did it consistently throughout his career. That's what people don't understand. It's not just about getting the players. It's about getting the players to play together as a unit. Phil made it cool for a player like me to defer and not get 20 points per game. He helped me see things in a way that I never had before. I totally sacrificed my ego and God blessed me with a ring. Earlier in my career I sought out the spotlight and the spotlight was great, but winning puts you in the brightest spotlight of all.

For the 2010–11 season, I took my old number 15 back. I thought of it as a way to finish off what I started. I was going to leave No. 37 with the 2010 championship season. Now it was time to get a ring for 15.

On opening night we received our championship rings before the start of the game, and I had already made plans for what I was going to do with my ring: I was going to raffle it off for charity. The cause that meant the most to me was mental health awareness, so that's where I wanted the money to go. I had been planning it for a while and I made sure the ring was a smaller size so it would better fit whoever won the raffle. When I first told my family about my plan, they were a little upset. They couldn't understand where I was coming from. Even some of my teammates thought it was crazy. I know Kobe said he would never give up his ring—he'd rather just give the money to charity and keep the ring.

But I wanted to do something positive with the ring. As you get older, your mind relaxes a little more. It becomes less about having fun and more about giving back. In the end, the ring wasn't what was important to me. It was the championship itself. I personally didn't need the ring to symbolize that accomplishment.

The online raffle was organized through my nonprofit Xcel University, so I could make sure that the money raised would be used to get more mental health therapists and services in community centers in New York, Los Angeles, Indiana, Cleveland, Little Rock, and Tennessee. It would help kids get the care they might not otherwise be able to afford. I wanted to make a difference in kids' lives and give them that extra push they might need to get past whatever they were struggling with. Most importantly, I wanted kids to realize that having mental health issues or family problems at home didn't mean something was wrong with them. They just needed some help.

I was a kid who would have benefited from that push. I carried my problems and scars from childhood with me all the way into the NBA. I was labeled a bad guy early in my career, but that had more to do with the environment I grew up in than who I was as a person. That's why I could relate to players like Dennis Rodman and those who struggled while growing up in a dysfunctional home. Instead of labeling people in those situations and turning them into villains, I found it was more productive to better understand the real issues so we could better deal with the problems. I needed answers because the issues were affecting me and my family. My scars didn't begin to heal until I went through counseling, and I knew that I wasn't the only one with those types of problems.

Even today, I want to let kids know that it's okay to seek help. It's nothing to be ashamed of. It's all about learning how to become comfortable with yourself. It doesn't matter if you're a professional athlete who is coming out as gay or a player who needs to seek help for a mental health issue. Be yourself, because you never want to be in a situation where you have to hide who you are. Holding things in creates unnecessary stress on your body and your mind. Releasing that stress by talking about it will make you feel better. Once I was able to speak openly about what I had been through, I wasn't afraid anymore. Instead, I felt powerful. I didn't care if the media called me crazy because I needed to see a psychologist. I was emotionally free and felt like nothing could stop me.

Being able to help kids experience that same feeling was what made raffling off the ring such an easy decision. The contest began the day after I got my ring. Tickets started at $2 with a minimum purchase of five tickets. It started off small, but when news spread things got out of control. It got a lot of attention in the media. The ring itself was worth about $26,000, but through the raffle we raised over $650,000 that we spread out between different mental health programs throughout the country. It went to help anyone who needed it—black, white, rich, or poor. We announced the winner on Christmas Day. We turned it into an event at the Conga Room, which was right across from the Staples Center. George Lopez was there to present the ring to the winner of the raffle, Raymond Mikhael. He was a father of four from Hawthorne. He bought 100 tickets and forgot about it. He didn't think he would actually win the ring, but then he got the call on Christmas morning.

I never set out to be a mental health advocate, but I had the chance to raise awareness and do a lot of good, so I helped out any way I could. I still consider raffling off my ring one of my biggest professional accomplishments, but the money I raised could only do so much. That's why I started doing speaking engagements.

In February of 2011, I traveled to Washington, D.C., to appear on a panel in support of the Mental Health in Schools Act, on behalf of California congresswoman Grace Napolitano. Speaking in front of a bunch of politicians was easy compared to getting up in front of hundreds of middle school kids at Eastmount Intermediate School back in Los Angeles. As soon as I got there, I stayed near the back. I picked at the food and drank the coffee. I felt so much better when Congresswoman Napolitano arrived. I think she knew I was nervous because she calmed me right down.

"What you're doing is more important than winning a championship," she said.

She was right. The cause was bigger than me and bigger than basketball.

Whenever I spoke in front of a group of people, I tried to talk about my own personal experience. I wasn't knowledgeable enough yet to speak about the medical side of mental health. It was an important issue and I didn't want people getting the wrong message from me. I also didn't want to deliver that message irresponsibly. I almost backed out of one of the engagements, but in the end I realized, who better to deliver that message than me? I was living proof that people could turn their lives around and become more positive while reaching their potential with the right professional help.

I never did any of that for the attention, but in April the NBA presented me with the J. Walter Kennedy Citizenship Award. It was nice to be recognized for doing something good after being criticized for so many years for doing things wrong. It wasn't one of the more glamorous awards, but it was one that was important to me because it was given to someone who "showed outstanding service and dedication to the community." That meant a lot to me and I valued it even more than my Defensive Player of the Year award.

I always secretly wanted the J. Walter Kennedy award. I never told anybody that. A few years earlier I never would have thought it would be possible for me to receive such an honor. From the moment I got into the league, I always gave back and tried to do something positive, but it felt like everything positive I did was wiped out by something negative. When people and the media would judge me, I always told them to wait for the end result because the story wasn't over yet. I knew I had to be more responsible and more professional. I had come such a long way, but it still felt that I had further to go before I become a role model.

When I thanked Dr. Santhi after Game 7, I had no idea it would touch so many people and lead me where it did. When I got the actual J. Walter Kennedy award, I wanted to put it up in Saladish, my restaurant in Pasadena, so people could come and see it. It was so easy to get wrapped up in the moment, but I couldn't take too much time to enjoy the award because before I knew it the Lakers were back in the playoffs.

Off the court my life was positive, but on the court that season went downhill fast and ended on a sour note when we got swept by the Mavericks in the second round. It was an ugly series and we didn't perform well. Our season was over, and that was also the end of Phil's coaching career. I wish we could have played better and sent Phil out on a high note, but we didn't execute. It was disappointing in every possible way. That season was the Mavericks' year. They went on to win the championship and we were left trying to figure out what went wrong.

That season we had six guys who played 82 games. Kobe, Fisher, Lamar, Luke, Pau, and Andrew had been to the Finals three years in a row. They played so many more games over that four-year period than most other players. We were healthy for a change and couldn't blame it on injuries, but playing all those games will catch up to anyone. By the time we got to Dallas, we had no legs. That's not an excuse because the Mavs beat us and proved they were the better team in that series. They deserved to win, and that was a humbling series. We knew that we had to come back stronger.

In spite of the loss, I was proud of our team. I would go into battle with those guys any time. There are so many great players in the league who never won a title or even got to the Finals, so even though we didn't three-peat, what that group accomplished together was pretty special.

Chapter 20

Give Peace a Chance

I had thought of changing my name for at least three years. I always liked to study history and black culture, but I had never come across any other Artests. My mom was a Holmes, but I didn't know anyone on my dad's side other than my aunt. I wanted to know exactly who I was and where I came from. Even my dad didn't know where the name Artest came from, so I decided to change my name to something that I identified with. It all went back to trying to be myself.

Plus, Ron Artest never missed an opportunity to entertain.

I had some crazy names picked out, but if I was going to actually go through with it and legally change my name, I wanted it to have meaning. I wanted to make an impact. I loved being inspirational and I had a lot of good things going on in my life. I had done a 180 in terms of my image and wanted to stay on the right path by being as positive as possible.

The idea for "World Peace" as my last name came first. That was a positive ideal that anyone on Earth could relate to. But I still needed a first name. For a while I was considering "One Love," but that was more of a tribute to Nas and didn't have the meaning I was looking for. So I got together with my team and we tried to think of a name with meaning. I decided that I wanted a name that would inspire people to do some research into what it meant. That's how we came up with "Metta."

Metta is a word that represents the Buddhist virtue of kindness. I'm not Buddhist—I grew up Baptist—but learning about meditation and other Buddhist principles had a positive impact on my life and helped me stay grounded. I also liked the idea that whenever my name was mentioned on television or during a game, it was spreading a positive message. I thought kindness and peace were better for people to hear about than guns, drugs, or violence. I wanted to get kids thinking bigger and about something positive for a change. You don't learn that in the hood and sometimes we need that spirituality.

I may have been changing my name but that didn't mean that I was going to change who I was. I wanted people to know that I took responsibility for the things I had done in the past, but that didn't mean I was suddenly a different person. I was still the same dude from the hood. I loved the streets. Nobody was going to suddenly see me turn away from who I was. This was about trying to improve and transform into the person I knew I could be.

In the end, picking out the name was a lot easier than actually changing it. My lawyer had to go to Los Angeles Superior Court and meet with a judge, but the official change was held up for a month because of an outstanding traffic ticket. After I paid the ticket, I officially became Metta World Peace. I had been Ron for 31 years so it definitely took some getting used to. It was weird when I heard people call me Metta out on the court. It took a little while to catch on and I was worried that I might have made a mistake, but pretty soon everyone started to embrace it. The public got attached to it.

The name change happened right before I was supposed to appear on season 13 of *Dancing with the Stars*. I didn't want to do the show at first. I wasn't much of a dancer but my daughter Diamond talked me into it. She was the real reason I went on the show. I had so much admiration for her personal strength that I couldn't say no.

Back in 2007, Diamond was diagnosed with cancer. She was four years old. I was playing in Sacramento, but Diamond was living with her mother in Indiana. It started as a belly ache. When Kimsha took her to the hospital, they found a tumor in her kidney and she was diagnosed with Stage 3 cancer. If she hadn't gone to the hospital when she did, it could have evolved into Stage 4.

Kimsha called me from the hospital and told me about the diagnosis. That was the worst day of my life. The fact that I was 2,000 miles away made it so much more difficult. I felt so helpless because there was nothing I could do. We had to stay positive, but it was in the hands of the doctors.

Normally doctors would remove the kidney given her condition, but Diamond was born with only one kidney to begin with. So, they tried to find a donor match while shrinking the tumor. She underwent chemotherapy and radiation. When it was time for the surgery, the doctors gave her a 90 percent chance of surviving, but that didn't ease my mind at all. Luckily they were able to remove the tumor while saving two-thirds of her kidney.

Once she recovered from the surgery, she became interested in music and came out with a single that described her experience called "Fighter." She even donated 15 percent of the profits from the song to St. Jude Children's Research Hospital, which was where she had the surgery.

We're so incredibly grateful that she's been healthy ever since. She was a tough soldier. Watching her go through that made me and Kimsha tougher. If my daughter could beat cancer, I could certainly handle *Dancing with the Stars*.

The rehearsals for that show were tough. My partner was Peta Murgatroyd, who had been on Broadway and was a professional Latin dancer. She was amazing. She taught me all about ballroom dancing and ballet, but I kept stepping on her feet. I was completely out of my element. I hadn't watched the show before so I didn't know what I was doing or what to expect.

I dyed my hair blond before the show. I didn't want to be some regular person out there. I was always trying to do something different to stand out, but it didn't work well that time. Peta and I were the first group to go out on the dance floor and we were the first group eliminated from the show. I made it one episode. If I had some more time to learn what I was doing, I think we could have gone further, but I missed some practices. It was fun, though. I got to meet some new people, including Rikki Lake and Nancy Grace, so I'm definitely glad I did it.

Being on the show also opened some doors for me. I later got a chance to act in a Lifetime movie based on Nancy's novel, *The Eleventh Victim*. I played a detective and starred alongside Jennie Garth. I got to do a few more movies, including a guest spot in *Think Like a Man*, with Kevin Hart. Acting was hard work and it took up a lot of time, but it was fun. I even had some reality shows in the works. Playing in L.A. allowed me to take advantage of all those different opportunities, but I had to be careful because they could easily become a distraction. Basketball was always the top priority.

Dancing with the Stars aired in September, and the only reason I could go on the show to begin with was because of the NBA lockout. There was a good chance there wouldn't be a season at all. We were looking at a possible nuclear winter. Since we weren't playing, I needed something do, but the lockout finally ended on December 8 and the first game of the season was scheduled for Christmas Day. I was looking forward to getting back to the chase for another championship, but I knew things were going to be very different for the Lakers in 2012.

We lost Lamar to Dallas in a trade and we also had a brand-new coach in Mike Brown following Phil Jackson's retirement. Mike and I went way back to our days in Indiana together. He had since taken the Cavs to the Finals as a head coach and was named NBA Coach of the Year. I loved Mike. I knew he was competitive and was a coach who stressed defense, so that would be good for the whole team.

Since the lockout didn't end until December, the schedule was reduced to 66 games that season. That put our team at a disadvantage because we had a whole new system to learn. For the first time since being a Laker, I actually had a leg up in that department because I had run that offense with Coach Brown before. There was still going to be an adjustment period, but it wouldn't be the same as trying to adjust to the triangle.

We came into our abbreviated training camp a little off, but that was the same challenge every team was facing. We were all rushing to get into shape. I had taken a couple months off in the summer, and I never took that much time off, so I had to work hard to get back up to speed. What hurt me was not being able to come into the Lakers facility to get treatment from trainer Garry Vitti. I had started to develop a problem with my Achilles during the previous year's playoffs and was getting treatment for it, but we had to stop when the lockout began.

On the court, I was hoping a different system would open up the offense for me, but it didn't. It never got easier. I had some career lows that year. I was averaging seven points per game on just 39 percent shooting from the field, but I was playing better by the end of the season. I was more aggressive and getting involved, but then came the incident that would forever taint that season for me. It's something that still haunts me.

I've made a lot of mistakes in my life, but I've learned from those mistakes and they helped me become a better player and a better person. I haven't done many things that I actually regret—there are only two. One of those regrets was the elbow I gave James Harden.

It happened during a game against the Thunder on April 22, 2012. It was the second-to-last game of the season. OKC had locked up the second seed in the West but we were still battling Memphis for the No. 3 spot, so it was a big game for us.

At the end of the second quarter, we were down 48–45. Bynum got a big block. He passed it ahead to me for a fast break. I had Durant one-on-one so I just took it at him. Kevin had no chance. Serge Ibaka was trailing, but I went up and dunked on both of them with my left hand.

That was my third big dunk of the game. I was feeling so good because I hadn't dunked like that in years. I was so hyped up, running on pure emotion and passion. I was pumping my chest and flexing to the crowd. I turned to run down the court when I bumped into James Harden, who was coming to get the inbounds pass. I didn't expect him to be right there. I swung my elbow in a "get off me" kind of way, but it was too much. I did not mean to hit him the way that I hit him, but I did and he went down hard.

Ibaka came after me, but both teams and the refs did a good job of breaking that up so nothing worse happened. I was ejected immediately.

At that moment, I didn't know that Harden was hurt and I didn't realize that I hit him as hard as I did. Then I saw the replay and cringed. That was a brutal elbow. The next day I found out that he suffered a concussion. Two days later, NBA commissioner David Stern suspended me for seven games. I thought seven games was excessive, but I didn't say anything about it. I took the suspension.

I received a lot of technical fouls throughout my career. I've been suspended, kicked out of games, and fined. I sat out an entire damn season and lost millions of dollars, but that was the first time I had ever hurt another player on the court. That was a different feeling. I'm glad that Harden was okay and would be able to play. If he had to sit out, or if the OKC playoff run was compromised because of something I did, that would have been awful. I never wanted something like that to happen. I never went out on the court looking to hurt anyone.

There was a good chance that we'd meet OKC in the playoffs so I didn't want to reach out to Harden personally. We were still competitors and I had to keep things competitive, so I reached out through a third party to make sure he was okay. When I found out that he would be fine and back in the lineup soon, I tried to move on. After the season I could talk with him personally. He was from the Los Angeles area. I saw him every once in a while and we played together, but for the time being I was focused on the playoffs.

My suspension meant that I had to sit out the first six games of our opening playoff series against the Nuggets.

That hurt because I was just finally getting into my rhythm. I was getting to the bucket. I was grabbing rebounds. I was on my A-game.

Without me, the Lakers went up 3–1 in the series, but the Nuggets battled back to tie it up and send it to a seventh game. I was excited to be back for Game 7. I didn't take my foot off the gas or change my game. If anything, I wanted to make sure that I stayed aggressive, so I went out there trying to be disruptive and to create as much havoc on the defensive end as I possibly could. I'll admit that I was exhausted. Most people don't realize how sitting out six games can affect you. You can practice and exercise all you want, but that's not the same as being in game shape. It took time to adjust. I played well in Game 7, but that was all heart.

We beat the Nuggets and that set up a series with OKC. It was bound to happen. The media bombarded me with questions about Harden, the suspension, and going to Oklahoma City, but I didn't address it. I stuck to my answers and tried to move on. The damage was done. I had to focus on the game and be able to go out there and be as competitive as possible.

As soon as we stepped out onto the floor for Game 1, those fans let me hear it. They were yelling. They had signs. It wasn't a surprise. Everybody knew they would come after me. I had been in that situation before so I was able to tune it out. I played hard. There were some scuffles in that series. I got tangled up with Westbrook in Game 3. At the end of the first half of Game 5, I fouled Thabo Sefolosha hard as he went in for a layup. I got mostly ball. A little body, but mostly I got the ball. They called it a flagrant foul. I wasn't going out there looking to prove anything, but it was important to me that I didn't change my game at all.

That series was a lot different from the series we played against the Thunder two years earlier. People were talking like we were on the decline and the Thunder were the new dynasty. They certainly played like that. They were the better team in that series. It was their time. Things were beginning to fall into place for the Thunder. They always had the players and the coaching, but now they also had the experience. Combine that with preparation, determination, and hard work, and that's what allows a team to advance in the playoffs.

In my mind we were still a great team. When we came together we were tough to beat. Bynum and Pau could do damage underneath the basket. We weren't supposed to lose. That wasn't supposed to happen. We were the team that was supposed to move on to the Western Conference Finals, but that was the second year in a row that we underachieved. We lost to OKC in five.

Our problem was on the offensive end. We turned the ball over too much. I also think we might have spent too much time looking to Kobe. It was easy to be in awe of Kobe and watch him take over the game. He had five championships. When we deferred to Kobe, it meant that the rest of the team made less of an impact. Guys had to believe in themselves and realize that they were on the team for a reason. Everyone had to do their part and not rely on one guy to carry the load. I was as much to blame for that as anyone else.

Mike Brown knew that the problem was offense. With new assistant Eddie Jordan on board for the 2012–13 season, Coach Brown decided that the Lakers were going to run the Princeton offense.

The team underwent another facelift before the start of the season. We acquired Dwight Howard, Steve Nash, and Antawn Jamison. Dwight had won Defensive Player of the Year three times and Nash had been MVP twice. Add Kobe to the mix and everyone was predicting a championship. Nash and Howard were on the cover of *Sports Illustrated*. I thought we'd go 73–9. How I arrived at that number, I don't really know. Expectations were high, but we didn't come close to living up to those expectations. We finished the year 45–37. Nobody predicted that.

That year was tough for the organization. I had never seen anything like that before. Everyone has a theory for what went wrong but the people who took the most heat were the coaches. After an 0–8 preseason and a 1–4 start to the regular season, Mike Brown was fired and replaced by Mike D'Antoni. Fans wanted Phil back, but the problem wasn't just the staff. Mike Brown and Mike D'Antoni were both good coaches, but nobody gave them a chance to coach, so they didn't have time to figure out how to best utilize their players. Everything was rushed. It was chaos.

At first we had to adapt to the Princeton offense, which was a great system if you had the right players, but it was not for everyone and it was definitely not suited for a team that revolved around Kobe Bryant. The weird thing about that offense was that it moved the superstar away from the ball. We didn't need our superstar away from the ball. We needed Kobe to be Kobe if we wanted to win. The triangle was perfect for Kobe.

We may not have adjusted well to the Princeton offense, but in our defense we weren't given any time to adjust. Then when D'Antoni replaced Mike Brown, we had to learn a completely different offense, and that was another one that didn't fit the team we had. It was a high-powered offense that involved ball movement. Everybody got a chance. It was equal opportunity. That's how the game should be played, but that meant another adjustment and one that didn't cater to our strengths as a team. Gasol, Howard, Jamison, and I could wear teams out in the post, but we were stuck running an offense that was all about moving off the ball, cutting, and shooting a lot of threes. Kobe was an on-the-ball player. He wanted the ball in his hands. It was in his DNA.

Of course, there were also the injuries. Dwight had back surgery in the off-season and had to sit out most of the preseason. Nash suffered a leg injury in the second game and missed seven weeks. Pau was hurt, and then Kobe tore his Achilles.

I had been lucky to avoid any serious injuries up to that point in my career. I'd had multiple surgeries on my thumb, but never something that threatened my career or had me out for an extended period of time. That year I was the only opening-day starter who had been healthy all season. Then, at the end of March, I went down with a knee injury. Luckily for me, it was only a torn meniscus and not an ACL. It did not require major surgery. Still, I was supposed to be out for six weeks, which could have meant the end of my season.

We were fighting to get into the playoffs. I felt bad. I knew it wasn't my fault, but it felt like I let the team down. I went online to learn the fastest that any player had ever come back from that type of injury. I read that some players were able to return in one or two weeks, so that was what I aimed for. I started doing rehab immediately after the surgery. It was usually the swelling that prevented you from playing after a knee procedure, and I was lucky enough not to have any swelling. That's how I was able to return to the lineup in 12 days.

We squeaked into the playoffs but were swept by the Spurs in the first round. It was a disappointing end to another season where we fell short of expectations.

A lot of people pointed the finger at Dwight and his relationship with Kobe, but I didn't think it was Dwight's fault. Dwight did well. He tried. He gave 100 percent, but he had a different personality and was not like the traditional franchise player. During the games he was focused, but off the court he was always happy and didn't take things too seriously. He was like a big teddy bear. He didn't have that killer instinct. He even told us that when he was younger everyone catered to him. He was given everything without having to work for it, so he had nobody there keeping it real with him. We tried to keep it real with Dwight. I only got to play with him for a year, but I did have a chance to get to know him. I respected Dwight because he acknowledged his limitations. One time he came right out and said that he got nervous when he went to the free throw line. To me, that was the first step in being able to improve. I respected him for coming out and saying that.

I think we put too much pressure on Dwight as a team. Pau and I should have been louder voices in the locker room. Kobe wanted me to be more of a vocal leader. At the time I wasn't comfortable doing that. Dwight wanted that role, but he wasn't equipped to do that for the Lakers yet. I was the older vet, so I should have pulled him aside and taken charge. Dwight may have been a superstar, but I had the experience and I had been there before. The problem was that I was never that guy on the Lakers. When I first got to L.A., I didn't say anything. I knew my place. I didn't do much talking. I'd listen to Fish and the other vets, but with Fisher gone I should have taken over that role. I should have helped Dwight and I feel bad that I did not talk to him about that.

The problem to me was bigger than any one player or any one issue. To me, the problem was that we never had any chemistry as a team. We had all these different pieces that were great on their own individually, but they never fit well together. The season was a disaster.

Before the season had even ended, there were rumors that I would be waived under the amnesty provision. That meant that the Lakers had to pay the remainder of my salary, but it wouldn't count against their salary cap. It wasn't personal, just another part of the game. I knew it was coming. Lakers general manager Mitch Kupchak gave me a call before the organization made it official and waived me in July of 2013.

Once again, I was looking for a new home.

NEW YORK

Chapter 21

Empire State of Mind

My basketball future was uncertain, but I never would have predicted what the next year had in store for me.

I didn't have to wait too long to find a new team. A few days after I was waived by the Lakers, I signed a two-year deal with the New York Knicks. I felt like a son coming home after being gone for 14 years. I had been back to Madison Square Garden a lot during my pro career, but the Garden hadn't been my home court since I played for St. John's back in 1999. Growing up in the city, I had that orange and blue in my blood. New York was where I wanted to finish out my career. The opportunity to do that meant a lot.

Some say that New York City is the hardest place to win. The Knicks haven't won a championship since 1973. Secretly, I always wanted to see the Knicks get their championship and now I had a chance to help them do that. I wanted to fight for the city.

When I was a kid, I dreamed of waking up in Queensbridge and taking the train to the Garden to play in an NBA game, so I decided that's what I was going to do. The night before my first game with the Knicks, I stayed in the hood and took the F train from the corner of 21st Street and 41st Ave. to Madison Square Garden. I had to make sure to go early enough because I wanted to get myself a seat and not be left standing up. That wouldn't be nearly as cool.

I wasn't home long before I realized how much had changed. Queens was now more similar to Manhattan. There were so many different people coming into the city. The area was growing; real estate was booming in locations that were almost abandoned 20 years earlier. It was an overwhelming experience for someone coming from a more laid-back setting in Los Angeles. Everyone in New York rushed around. It was hectic. People were loud and in your face. I wasn't like that anymore. I had worked so hard to control my emotions and break some of those aggressive habits that I developed on the streets. I'll always be hood, but I was a different type of person. It wasn't until I came back home that I realized how much I had grown.

I wanted to relax and take my time that year, but it was difficult. My sister Shalice had been battling cancer for a few months, and right before the start of training camp I learned that she wasn't going to survive. Shalice took care of me when I was younger. Now, I was watching her pass away. It was heartbreaking for me and it was even more heartbreaking for her eight children. I had to be there for them. I was grateful to be in the city so I could see her and spend time with her.

Watching her fight cancer was an inspiration to me. Death reminds you how fragile life is. It reminded me that there are so many things more important than basketball. I had been through that before, when Quanisha died. The emotions I felt at Shalice's funeral were the same I experienced when I was a teenager. No matter how much I had matured or grown, dealing with the death of a family member took the same toll on me emotionally. That will never get easier. Luckily, I had my family with me. Knicks president Steve Mills and assistant GM Allan Houston both showed up at Shalice's funeral. I wasn't expecting that, but I definitely appreciated their support.

It was hard to focus on basketball, but I had a job to do. That job was made even more difficult because of my knee. I hadn't given it a chance to completely heal after surgery the previous year. I rushed my recovery because I thought I could help the Lakers make the playoffs. That wasn't the smartest thing for me to do and I was paying for it now. I had developed a Baker's cyst in my knee that gave me a lot of problems. I had to have it drained five times and I was starting to miss some games. That made it clear there was something wrong, so in January I decided to undergo platelet-rich plasma treatment. It was the same procedure that guys like Kobe, Tiger Woods, and Alex Rodriguez had gotten. Even my teammate A'mare Stoudemire had it done and it seemed to work well for him.

PRP is different from surgery. It's an injection of your own blood that has been enriched with platelets in order to heal the tendon and reduce the swelling. That was the medical definition, at least.

I had made calls and prepared to go all the way to Germany, but I found a doctor who could do it for me right there in New York. The procedure was not approved by the FDA, but it could still be administered in the U.S. by doctors who were properly trained in the technology. Since it wasn't a surgery, there were no special licenses required.

The doctor numbed my knee with Novocain and then injected the blood platelets. An ultrasound was hooked up so the doctor could make sure the needle went into the tendon. It didn't hurt. It just felt weird. That eventually went away, but it wasn't a miracle cure. I still needed time to recover, so I sat out two weeks. I couldn't afford to be macho by rushing back. I was going to work with trainer Roger Hinds to make sure that I was 100 percent before I returned.

As a vet who had been there before and won a championship, it felt like it was my job to get that team ready for the playoffs. In L.A., we pushed ourselves. We weren't afraid to speak up or get into it with each other. We went hard. We were at each other's throats when the situation called for it. That's how we got ready for the game, but that Knicks team was much more cautious around each other. It was not the same atmosphere.

Ever since I was a kid, I always let my teammates know if they weren't playing defense. That was one of my pet peeves, because if you didn't give effort and you didn't play defense, you wouldn't win in the playoffs. If Carmelo Anthony was playing lazy defense, I spoke up, because we'd find ourselves going home early if we didn't fix those problems. After one game, I got into it with J.R. Smith in the locker room. I got on him for his effort and his defense. I might have been too direct. I wasn't trying to call him out. It all came from a good place. J.R. took offense at first but he understood where I was coming from. J.R. and I have always been cool and recently we played on the same team in the Drew League.

I may have been hard on J.R., but that's because he had so much potential. He was having a pretty good year, as was Iman Shumpert. With those guys playing so well, I wasn't getting much time. I don't know how well I fit in with that Knicks team. They moved the ball up the court and shot from the perimeter. I was hoping to bring some toughness inside, but I never felt like I got a fair shot in New York. Even so, I didn't want to question coach Mike Woodson. I wondered why he wasn't playing me, but I had to let him be the coach.

My contract was for two years, but if I wasn't playing my first year in New York, I knew that I wouldn't play my second year. I wanted to be in New York. It was great to be home and I loved the chance to play in front of the New York fans. It's not that I wasn't happy. I wanted to win there, but I also wanted to play. I only had so many years left in me and I knew that I could still make an impact. I didn't want to spend that time on the bench.

I first started discussing a trade with my agent and the Knicks front office in December. That was before I had my knee procedure. The problem was that I didn't want to be a distraction or take any blame for disrupting the team. When the Knicks came out in January to win six of their first seven games, it felt like a good time for me to leave. We negotiated a buyout and I was officially waived on February 24. I was once again a free agent.

WORLDWIDE WORLD PEACE

Chapter 22

The Panda's Friend Goes to China

I didn't feel like I had been playing the way that I was capable of playing. I had been a role player for so long that it felt like I lost my individual offensive game. I wanted to go somewhere where I could get that back, and the best place to do that wasn't in the NBA at all. There was some talk of me joining the Clippers to finish the season, but in July I signed a deal to play with the Sichuan Blue Whales in the Chinese Basketball Association.

When you grow up playing basketball in the city, it's easy to forget that it's a big world and a lot of other countries love basketball. I went from playing in my own backyard to the other side of the globe. Sichuan was one of the wealthier teams in the CBA. I met with two other Chinese teams, but I signed with Sichuan because they seemed like the best fit for me.

I had talked to my agent about playing in Greece before I signed with the Lakers back in 2009. I was always interested in traveling the world. My old teammate, Bonzi Wells, had played in China and he told me how fun it was. Stephon Marbury had been playing there for years and was treated like a god. There is a statue of Stephon in Beijing and he has his own postage stamp. They even opened up a Stephon Marbury museum. It goes to show how much the fans love basketball. Not every player who went to China was successful; Steve Francis, Kenyon Martin, Gilbert Arenas, and even Tracy McGrady all briefly played in China, but didn't last very long for whatever reason. But I was willing to give it a shot.

My international career didn't get off to a great start. On my very first day in China, I got so incredibly sick that I had to be hospitalized for three days. All I'm going to say is that the hospitals in China are different from American hospitals, but thankfully I recovered. When I got out, I made sure to have my food shipped to me from Hong Kong and the United States. I was on a very strict diet at the time, but it was hard for me to find a lot of the raw vegan food I was eating. When I moved out of the hotel I was staying in and into an apartment, I could finally start cooking for myself. I had no choice but to become a good cook. It was important that I learned how to cook and it was also important that I learned how to say "mayo," which is the Chinese word for "no." Very, very important.

One of the reasons Marbury did so well in China was because he embraced the culture and the people. I wanted to do the same, so I started telling people on Twitter that I was going to change my name again. I decided that if I was going to change my name for the second time, I wanted my new name to be something that reflected my new home. The panda was the most famous animal in the Sichuan province, and every time my daughter Sade saw a panda, she would cry because she loved them so much. That touched me. The thing I liked about the panda was that it was strong and it defended its territory, but it was also laid-back and calm. I thought that really fit who I was, and that's how I came up with "The Panda's Friend." I never actually changed my name, but it got so much press that I just kind of went with it. The name did become the inspiration for my clothing line. On the court, I wore shoes that had a removable panda's head on the tongue. It was like a pom-pom. I'd throw the panda's head into the crowd and tell everyone that the person who caught it would be the panda's friend for a day.

Living in China required some adjustment. The lifestyle in the CBA was very different from the NBA lifestyle I was used to. The first thing that stood out was the travel. In the NBA you flew private, but in China you flew commercial and carried your own bags. You did everything with the team. You ate all your meals together. You stretched together. You practiced together. You all walked around in the same warmup outfit together. Being together with everyone on the team could get difficult at times, but in the long run it was good for developing team chemistry.

Also, the talent in the Chinese league wasn't evenly distributed. The top four teams were really good, but there was a big drop-off after that. I quickly learned that I had to adjust my game as well. China was a physical league, but they played a very different style of basketball. It was much less structured than the NBA. The one person I would call the most for advice was Phil Jackson. I'd ask him things like how to beat a zone defense. He also helped me figure out how to play with teammates who were not fundamentally sound. A lot of my teammates couldn't make a post pass. They wouldn't be able to throw an alley-oop or hit me when I cut back door.

Phil would tell me things I could do to help them succeed, so I spent a lot of my time in China working with the other players and coaching them up in practice.

It was difficult to dominate in the league because of that lack of structure, but I still had a pretty good year. I averaged 19 points and was shooting 42 percent from the field, but my knee became a problem for me again. I only played 15 games and had to sit out the rest of the season.

The one thing that stood out the most to me about professional basketball in China was the fans. They were absolutely amazing. I had fans show up at the airport to greet me when I first arrived. The NBA may get 30 million people watching the Finals, but in China they'll get something like 300 million people. They love basketball, but the CBA was a couple steps behind the NBA when it came to marketing. Hardly any of the stadiums sold jerseys at the games. The league hadn't figured out how to sell the game right yet, but once it does basketball can become even bigger there.

I loved China. The experience was incredible and the fans were so supportive, but after living there for five months it was time for me to move on. The plan was always for me to return to the NBA somehow, but another opportunity presented itself first and it was one that I couldn't turn down.

I wasn't joking around when I said that I would play in Europe. I don't think anybody took me seriously when I first brought up the idea, not even my agent, but in March of 2015 the Italian league was winding down and teams were looking to make a playoff run. I got the opportunity to play with Pallacanestro Cantu, so I signed a contract to finish out the season. Cantu was in 10th place out of 16 teams. They had to make it into the top eight to qualify for the playoffs. We only had eight games left, but I liked the challenge. I would rather play for a team that was making a playoff push and help get them over the hump than join a contender that was already there.

One of the reasons I wanted to play in Europe was because they moved the ball and played team basketball. In Europe, you were encouraged to play with your teammates. There were no isolations like there were in the NBA. I loved playing like that. It was fun. I knew a lot of guys who had played in Italy and been successful. Eric Chatfield had been all over Europe and had recently made a name for himself in Italy. Both Bootsy Thornton and Tyrone Grant from St. John's had played in Italy and did really well.

It was pretty much a sink-or-swim situation for me. I hadn't played basketball since November and I was jumping into a situation where I'd be playing for a new team in a new country during the middle of the season. There wouldn't be any training camp or any time to get adjusted. I don't think I slept at all the first two nights after I arrived. I was able to jump in and find my groove with the team right away, but there just weren't enough games left in the season. I would have liked to have played more, but I felt like I accomplished what I was there for. I had a lot of great highlights and even ended my season in Italy with an ejection, so I like to think the fans in Italy got the whole Metta World Peace experience.

I loved Italy and want to go back to Cantu someday. They had the best pasta. The fans were great and the country was filled with beautiful people. Being able to play basketball in other countries and experience other cultures was something I enjoyed tremendously. If the opportunity presented itself I would love to do it again. The one place I really want to go and play ball is Africa, so hopefully I'll be able to do that someday.

All that said, there was never any doubt that the best players in the world played in the NBA. I needed to get back home.

LOS ANGELES

Chapter 23

I Love L.A.! Vol. 2

had been out of the NBA for almost two years, but I knew that I could still be productive. I had the respect of the NBA players. I crossed paths with a lot of them during the summers and they knew I could still play. When I got back to my home in L.A., I played everywhere. I was down in Venice Beach. I was over in Calabasas. I was playing at Equinox when I went there to work out.

But getting back into the NBA was not going to be easy. There are only 400 spots in the league and they aren't easy to come by. I would have to earn it just like I had 17 years earlier. It was like I had to start all over again. My agent asked me, "Are you sure you want to go through this again?" I was all in, so my agent and I reached out to let teams know that I was ready to play.

A lot of teams thought I was still hurt; some thought I was too outspoken in the locker room. Everyone was telling me that my career was over. Not many teams wanted to take a chance on me.

I didn't let it be known to the media, but I knew where I wanted to play. I wanted to stay in Los Angeles. I may not have played for the Lakers for a couple of seasons, but I never left L.A. I lived in Westwood. It was home to me. Most importantly, they knew me in L.A. better than in any other city. I followed the Lakers when I was in China and Italy. I texted with Kobe often. It was all about that purple and gold.

The Lakers were my only real option. I'm sure it wasn't easy to convince Mitch Kupchak to take a chance on me, but the Lakers signed me to a one-year, non-guaranteed contract. That didn't mean I was on the team yet. The Lakers invited 19 players to training camp, but they could only keep 15 on the final roster. I had to work hard and prove that I belonged there. I didn't want it any other way. I didn't want anybody to hand me anything. However, I had never been in the position of having a non-guaranteed contract. That was new to me. It was stressful, but I stayed patient and played my game. I was dedicated. I was ready. I had taken care of my body. I still trained hard, but now I trained smarter.

Byron Scott was in his second year as head coach and his training camp was tough. I busted my ass during camp and also found myself in the strange position of helping to teach some of the same young players I was trying to beat out for a roster spot. I'd be sure to coach them up when I could, but when I went up against them, I'd bust their ass.

Players today need to work on the simple things in the game, like back-door passes and setting screens. It's all about fundamentals. A lot of the young studs think they're better than they are. They don't listen right away. It takes some time for them to be humbled and come back down to earth. That's when they're ready to listen to criticism. It's the small things that win you a championship. If I could do anything, I wanted to instill in those young guys the mindset of a winner.

When camp was over, I had made the team. I made the fucking team! Not many people gave me a chance, but I was ready to play. I was going to play hard and give great effort, but I was also going to enjoy myself and keep it simple. I was a different player out on the court. I had finally learned how to control my emotions. I didn't hold on to those frustrations. When the refs missed a call, I'd be pissed for a couple seconds and then snap out of it. I didn't mind being punked anymore. If someone got up in my face, I walked away. It wasn't worth it.

Kobe was still the leader, but the Lakers were a young team. I couldn't wrap my head around how young some of those guys where. D'Angelo Russell was the same age as my oldest daughter. I knew that my role would be reduced, but I was okay with that. When I came up in the league, I had guys like Reggie Miller helping me. There were so many players who reached out to me and tried to help me when I was younger. If I had listened to them back then, my career might have turned out differently. Now it was my turn to steer the young guys down the right path so they wouldn't make the same mistakes that I did. I had to put aside my ego again to be a supportive teammate and do what I could to help those guys win.

My career had officially run the gamut. I had gone from being the number one guy on a contender to the fourth or fifth option off the bench. Now, I was the 15th guy on the team. I was the last one to make the roster.

I thought back to that 2010 championship team. Adam Morrison was a guy going hard in every practice. He'd talk trash and he'd back it up, but he rarely got in games. Josh Powell was another guy who was a huge part of that team. He was very vocal during our film sessions, but nobody knew about his contribution outside of the team. Those guys motivated the rest of us. They got us ready to play. I saw firsthand how much guys like that could help a team and that's what I had to do for these young Lakers.

The coaches wanted to develop the rookies and get them lots of playing time, but I made sure I was 100 percent ready when my number was called. I never let playing time influence my effort or prevent me from being ready. Plus, the reality was I was 36 years old and I had been out of the league for two years. At first, I was worried that I might not be able to guard some of the younger guys, but I proved to myself and everyone else that I could still compete physically once I got out there.

In October, before the season even started, I received some terrible news. The Lakers were in Las Vegas getting ready for a preseason game when I learned that Lamar Odom had been hospitalized and was in a coma. I didn't know what to make of that news when I heard it. Lamar had been out of the league for a few years and I knew he had been going through a difficult time, but I still couldn't believe what I was hearing. I broke down crying.

I love Lamar. He's so outgoing, charismatic, and likeable that everyone wants to be around him. He's a caring person and a good friend, probably a better friend than me. I was always bad at keeping in touch with people because I always had so much going on in my life. I had bumped into Lamar earlier that summer. We talked about training together, but we never had the chance to meet up and do it. I wish I could have reached out and done something to help him.

Kobe and I were the only ones on the current Lakers team who played with Lamar. Kobe was just as upset as I was and he flew out to visit Lamar. Mitch Kupchak visited. The Lakers organization showed its support. My brother Daniel tried to visit Lamar. They wouldn't let him in the hospital at first, so he checked into the hotel across the street. I spoke to a lot of my friends back home who grew up with Lamar. His former coaches Artie Cox and Vincent Smith also reached out.

I was bitter for the next couple of days. I came down really hard on the Kardashians. I'm not even really sure why, but I was looking for someone to blame for my friend being in the hospital and on his deathbed. It wasn't fair of me to blame them but I felt powerless. There was nothing I could do but hope for the best and wait to see if he was going to pull through.

Our trainer Gary Vitti was the one who kept us updated on Lamar's health. It was a long road back but slowly he improved. Khloe did her thing and stuck by his side. I know that she was able to help Lamar. I think she's the one who brought him back to life and I'm grateful to her for that. What's funny is that Khloe met Lamar at my "Welcome to L.A." party back in 2009. They were married seven days later.

Lamar was really into that L.A. lifestyle. He was an entertainer, but I'd like to see him get into coaching. He was such a smart player and he always had great energy; I can picture him using that energy to teach kids about the game. No matter what he ends up doing, I will support Lamar through thick and thin. I will always be there for him.

The news about Lamar was a rough way to start the season, and it didn't get much better from there. We won only 17 games all year. Everyone knew there would be growing pains, but I think we all had higher expectations. I felt that it was my job to try and pull the team together when some of the younger guys wanted to point fingers at each other.

In their frustration, the fans blamed Byron Scott. It had been a couple years since the Lakers were the dominant franchise that everyone was used to. I think the fans were growing impatient, but it wasn't Byron's fault. Byron wasn't the one out there on the floor. He wasn't the one missing shots. Dealing with such a young team was not easy either. Byron was under a lot of pressure that season. I know other coaches who would have given up, but Byron kept pushing us all the way to the end. That season was extra hard on Byron because it was also Kobe Bryant's final season.

At the end of November, Kobe announced that he was retiring after 20 years with the Lakers. He wrote a poem about how he fell in love with the sport as a kid. He posted it online and distributed a letter to every fan before the start of a Sunday game at Staples Center. I made sure to get a copy of that poem and I had Kobe sign it for me. He wrote, "Love you like a brother forever." I put that in a frame and hung it on my wall.

People gave Kobe a bad rap from time to time. They said he wasn't social enough or that he didn't always sign autographs for the fans. Kobe gave every bit of his soul to the game. If he wasn't accessible, it was because he was so focused on basketball and winning. It wasn't until after he retired that I really got the chance to talk with him about something other than basketball. He's made his mistakes, but that's because he was never a god, no matter how much some people wanted to see him as one. He was a human being who was a great basketball player.

Kobe was a blessing to me. He's the one who helped me get my ring. I dreamed of winning an NBA title since I was a kid, and without Kobe Bryant that wouldn't have been possible. He was the one who passed me the ball at the end of Game 7. He could have taken that shot or passed it to somebody else, but he shared it with me. That moment changed my life. Being able to win an NBA title with Kobe Bryant by my side—it doesn't get much better than that.

The rest of the season was basically Kobe's retirement tour and he filmed the whole thing for a documentary. Kobe was a competitor and wanted to finish strong. He wanted to give the fans something to remember him by, and he did just that when he dropped 60 points against the Jazz in the last game of his NBA career. No script could have been written that would have topped what Kobe did that night. I thought he'd get around 30 points because I knew he would play hard. Kobe surpassed everyone's expectations. Even Kobe couldn't have planned for that. For him to go out the way he did was incredible.

Everybody knew how important that game was for Kobe. In the locker room before tipoff, he gave a speech about going out there and playing hard. That was when I started to feel the emotion. I was so motivated to go out there and play, but I never got in the game. I would have loved to be out there, but I was still the most excited guy in the arena. That night was about Kobe, not about me.

That game was the closest we had to a championship that season. It didn't look like it was going to be his night, and we were down 15 at halftime, but then Kobe caught fire. For the Lakers to win and for Kobe to drop 60 in his final game, it felt like we just won a championship. He told me that he didn't want champagne. He was very hard to impress, especially when it came to his own performance.

"I only drink champagne when we win championships," he said.

Brandon Bass, Lou Williams, and I got him champagne anyway. After that game, the energy in the arena reminded me of what it felt like to win a ring, but it only lasted for five minutes. Everyone quickly came back down to earth and realized that Kobe was through and we were out of the playoffs. Still, it was such a special night for the entire city, and I'm glad I got to be a part of that. Even from the bench, it was emotionally draining.

I believe Kobe is the best player of his generation. Tim Duncan is close because he's got five rings, too. I'd also give Kobe the edge over LeBron, and maybe even Jordan, but it's so hard when you try to compare players from different eras. Jordan does have one more ring than Kobe. I grew up a Michael Jordan fan, but he was at the end of his career by the time I got to the league. Kobe was only a year older than me, so I got to watch him evolve. Then, when I got to the Lakers, I was able to see him every single day.

Kobe was extremely tough. He could do everything. He had every move. He could shoot, go right, go left, fade away, and even hit the three. He could go by you or over you. He was very athletic and that made him hard to play against. Kobe and Jordan had similar games. If you watch them closely, they have the same exact moves.

Who was the hardest player for me to guard? That's the question people always ask me and it's not easy to answer. There are so many good players, but the two guys who consistently had good games when I guarded them were Kobe and LeBron. I had some good wins when we went head to head, but they each had more wins than me when I guarded them. I felt like I got the better of most all of the other superstars in the league, but Kobe and LeBron were the two most difficult players for me to guard.

The reason LeBron was so difficult for me was because he passed the ball. It would be so much easier to guard LeBron if he was a selfish player. A player like Carmelo Anthony was easier for me personally, because I didn't have to worry as much about helping out. Durant was also a tough cover because he moved so much. One of the up-and-coming guys I didn't have the chance to play against in my prime was Kawhi

Leonard. He was difficult for the same reasons LeBron was, but I only matched up against Kawhi at the beginning of his career when he was just starting to emerge.

After the regular season ended, I had to take stock of where I was at in my career. I had grabbed the final roster spot on a 17-win Lakers team, and now Kobe was retired. If my run in the NBA was at an end, I was hoping to go out on my own terms.

Chapter 24

Positivity Not Negativity

I wanted to play 20 professional seasons. That was my own personal goal. I had just finished my 18th season, but I was under a one-year contract, so I had to wait and see if the Lakers were going to invite me to camp in 2016–17. If there was a spot for me to earn, I was going to go out there and earn it. If that didn't work out, I was going to take my show on the road. I had a streetball team called "The Pandas" that I planned to travel with and play some games around the world.

In the meantime, I did what I always did. My role may have been that of a mentor and a veteran leader, but during the summers I was in the gym. I always worked on becoming a better basketball player. That's what I did when I was 16, it's what I did when I was 26, and it's what I did when I was 36. That never changed.

It was a great relief to be invited to Lakers training camp at the start of the 2016 season with new coach Luke Walton.

Luke had been an assistant at Golden State and had a great run when he filled in for Warriors head coach Steve Kerr to start the previous season. Luke was on our Lakers championship team in 2010. I may have been older than him by a couple of months, but he always had my back when I got to L.A. I used to ask him a ton of questions and he helped me learn the system. He didn't always play much, but when he was in there he could get five quick assists and change the game without scoring. That's hard to do. Back then I used to tell him that he should be a coach, but he didn't seem interested at the time.

Twenty players were invited to camp to compete for 15 spots. I was in the same boat as the previous year with another one-year, non-guaranteed contract. A lot of people in the media thought it was unlikely that I'd make the team in 2015, but in 2016 absolutely nobody gave me a chance. I made sure that I showed up to camp in shape and I played hard. I had taken care of my body over the off-season, eating right and staying away from alcohol. That's what gave me the chance to run with those young guys. It came down to the very last cut, but once again I proved everybody wrong and earned that last spot on the 2016 Lakers roster.

My role was very similar to the previous year, but just because I was the veteran didn't mean that I didn't have anything to learn. In fact, I think I learned just as much from those young guys as they learned from me. They also made me feel young again. I was doing things in the locker room and on the road that I hadn't done in years. I enjoyed myself in ways that I didn't when I was younger, back when I had so much dysfunction going on in my life.

I had come to appreciate the time I had spent in the league. I tried to make the most out of every game and every road trip. When we went to Indiana, I made sure to speak with

Pacers media relations director David Benner. I wanted to apologize for all that I put him through when I played there. I still feel bad about how things ended in Indiana and I want to see the Pacers win a championship one day. That might help me feel a little better about things.

The 2016 season was also the last year that the Pistons would play at the Palace of Auburn Hills before they moved into a new arena in downtown Detroit. Right after the brawl I feared going back to Detroit, but now I love it. I love the fans. Every time I walked into that building, I got flashbacks. I liked to go into the arena when it was empty and there were no fans. When I looked out onto the court, over to the scorer's table, and up into the stands, the events would all play out right before my eyes as though they happened yesterday.

It's not just the arenas that are changing. Most of the guys I came into the league with back in 1999 are no longer playing. I've been a professional basketball player for almost half of my life. I'm blessed that I was able to play for so long because I should have been out of the league a long time ago, but I was able to get it together and stay focused in spite of my instabilities. I'm proud of myself for that. Things got tough. When I was depressed, I didn't let myself stay down. When I came into camp out of shape, I made sure to get back down to my playing weight. If I got hurt, I fought to get back on the court as quickly as possible. I kept getting up and always bounced back.

However, my career was never where I wanted it to be. I had very high standards when it came to my own performance, and when I look back over my career I see a lot of missed opportunities. I played in only one All-Star Game. I was named Defensive Player of the Year only once and I won just one NBA championship. Those are great achievements, but when

I was in my prime I felt that I was the best two-way player in the league. I could have won that Defensive Player of the Year award a couple more times. Had I stayed in Indiana, I think I could have been an All-Star a few more times and I believe we would have won an NBA championship. But it's my own fault that I didn't live up to that potential. I couldn't stay out of trouble. I wasn't a good teammate. I didn't always take care of my body the way I should have. I hurt my team with all the flagrant fouls and the fines and the suspensions. Add all of those things up and they tarnished my legacy. I could have done so much more.

My behavior also cost me a shot at the Olympics. I wanted a gold medal so badly, but I never got a chance to try out for Team USA. Years ago I even called Jerry Colangelo, who runs USA Basketball, but he hung up on me. I wanted to be able to represent my country in the Olympics and I'm still a little salty about not being given that opportunity.

In spite of the disappointments, I don't regret how things have played out. The mistakes I made were necessary for me to grow into a stronger person. I mentioned earlier that I only had two regrets. The first was elbowing James Harden. The second was not being there 100 percent for my wife. Kimsha and I are divorced now. I fucked that up. I was a bad partner and a bad husband. It cost me my marriage and that's a major regret, but I'm lucky that Kimsha and I are still best friends. We had some of the craziest fights, but we've come a long way and been through so much that we trust each other and work together as parents.

I'm thankful that Kimsha has allowed the kids to come live with me. It's great to be at home with my children. I understand how to raise a family now and I'm a better parent than I ever was before. I love cooking breakfast and dinner for the family. Being there for my kids is a great feeling. My oldest daughter wants to be a chef and loves to cook, so that's something we do together. Not only is she grown up and out of the house, but she's also pregnant. Her baby is due in April of 2018, so by the time you are reading this I will be a grandfather. That's crazy to me and I still haven't wrapped my head around that, but I'm excited. My youngest daughter is interested in cheerleading and dance while my two sons play basketball. That's what led me to coaching.

It started with me being an assistant who helped out with my sons' AAU and high school teams. I never thought about being a coach but I was always a student of the game. As I got older, I found myself helping other players and listening more to what my coaches were trying to teach me. I learned so much from all of my coaches and I've played for some of the best. I've learned to pay attention to the details. I can identify when a player is being too emotional or playing selfishly, because I've hurt teams that I was on by doing both. I know defense. I know basketball is not just a physical game. I know when not to talk to the players and allow them to learn from their mistakes. I can also pass along one of the most important lessons I learned, and that is how to play the game relaxed. Those Spurs teams with Tim Duncan were the perfect example. They didn't showboat or show emotion, but they won because they were fundamentally sound, they played as a team, and they were relaxed.

I love to coach. It doesn't matter what level. My dad and I run a basketball camp in New York City to work with some of the younger kids. I wish we could have done more things like that earlier in our lives, but it's cool that my dad and I finally get to do stuff like that now. A few years ago, I coached the Palisades High girls basketball team. We won back-to-back titles. One year we started the season 3–10 but won 20 games in a row to win a title. When I coach, I put the systems

269

that I was taught in place. It's so exciting to see a play unfold just like I drew it up. I provide instruction and let the kids run with it. Today, I really get to put my skills as a coach to the test because in October of 2017, I accepted a job as a development coach with the South Bay Lakers in the NBA's Gatorade League. I'm not making nearly the kind of money I was as a player, but I love being a part of the game. I like to think of this as just the beginning. I still have a long way to go as a coach, but I'm eager to learn and work my way up the ladder just as I did as a player.

After all these years, I'm still learning things on and off the court. I'm okay with making mistakes. I still make a lot of them, but I know that I'm going to get through it. I still see my psychologist, because I want to keep improving and learning more. We have to keep working on ourselves and we all need a support system. The trick is to work at it. It doesn't happen overnight. Nothing changes that fast. It's a process. Everything takes time, whether it's getting off drugs, building a business, or trying to become a great basketball player. It all takes time, so I try to enjoy the journey.

My mission is still to give back and that's something I always plan to do. I used to fear public speaking or getting up in front of a group of kids, but now a part of me gets off on being able to speak about a great cause. I've spoken to the inmates at San Quentin and I've spoken to at-risk youths. One place I love to talk is in Detroit. For the past couple of years, I've spoken at the schools in Detroit whenever the Lakers rolled into town. There is so much that needs to be done in that city. I drive through the streets and see the abandoned buildings. I've been working on ideas for programs that can help the city of Detroit. There are kids growing up there who went through the same things that I went through, so if I can talk to those kids and reach them, hopefully we can begin to improve the situation in that city. I know the challenges those kids face. I understand their struggles. I know how easy it is to sell drugs or go down the wrong path when you need to support yourself and your family. It's hard to get people to change because so many kids have been programmed by their environment. We've got kids thinking that they'll never be able to graduate high school, so they give up without even trying. That's why I tell them my story and hopefully show them that there is another way.

There are a lot of black players in the NBA who grew up like me and didn't come from a background where they were exposed to the world of business. My parents were always trying to find jobs and work for other people, instead of being able to work for themselves. I didn't have the educational background that prepared me to own anything. I sometimes wish that I stayed at St. John's to earn a degree in economics or business, so I would have the background and knowledge to better run my business. I had to learn that as I went along. That's why I encourage players to take their education seriously and get their degree, so they have something to fall back on when they can no longer play basketball.

The harsh reality is that nobody can collect an NBA check forever. My playing career has come to an end, but I had my check taken away from me after the brawl. I learned to appreciate the privilege of playing in the league. I learned that things can change in the blink of an eye and that nothing is guaranteed. Those early mistakes prepared me to make the transition to this next chapter of my life.

No matter what happens in the future, I want to make sure that my time is working for me and not against me. I want to be able to enjoy myself and not be serious all the time. Even though I'm focused on coaching now, I'm still going to play ball whenever there is a basketball and a hoop. There are hundreds of thousands of hoops all over the world, so I'll have plenty of opportunities. Wherever I am and whatever problems I'm faced with, I'll continue to search for solutions. You can count on that.